Field Guide to
Trees
and Shrubs
of Britain and Europe

How to identify trees and shrubs

> **Needle leaves**
> **Pages 26 – 51**

This section contains woody plants with needle-shaped leaves, such as the Silver Fir, Spruce, Pine, Yew and Cedar.

> **Pinnate leaves**
> **Pages 52 – 77**

This section contains woody plants with pinnate (feathery) leaves, such as the Scotch Broom, Stag's Horn Sumach, Mountain Ash and Horse-Chestnut.

> **Tree or shrub?**

A tree is a woody plant which has a recognisable trunk, free of branches up to a certain height. The trunk can attain a large girth and great height. A tree has a crown of branches and twigs. In some trees, the trunk grows continuously and perfectly upright through-out its life. In others, the trunk divides into several thick branches, sometimes not far above the ground.

2

➤ **Simple, opposite leaves**
Pages 78 – 105

This section contains woody
plants with simple leaves,
arranged facing each other,
such as Lilac, Cornelian
Cherry and Maple.

➤ **Simple, alternating leaves**
Pages 106 – 185

This section contains woody
plants with simple, alternating
leaves, for example Alder,
Poplar, Oak and Willow.

Shrubs, on the other hand, do not have a continuous, clearly-
defined trunk, and divide just above ground level into several
stems of roughly similar thickness. Shrubs can also branch straight
from ground level.

A significant number of woody plants, such as the Hawthorn,
Elderberry and Lilac, can be found both in shrub form or as a small
tree, depending on the growing conditions of the particular habitat.

Step-by-step identification

Wild Cherry
Prunus avium

DESCRIPTION: A deciduous tree which can grow to a height of 30m and has a very regular, tapering or round crown ①. Older trunks have smooth bark with horizontal, warty bands around them ②. The loose bark can be rolled up in horizontal st...

LEAVES: Stemmed ... ves end in a short point ③. Edges have ...-pointing serration.

BLOOMS: Five-petalled flowers arranged in groups of two to five on shorter branches.

FRUITS: The cherries hang on long stems from branches ④. Change colour from yellow to red to almost black when ripe.

DISTRIBUTION: Deciduous and mixed woodland, but also woodland edges and hedgerows.

OTHER: Cultivated sweet cherries originate from the Wild Cherry. Its fruits are edible, but are slightly bitter. Unlike the Bird Cherry (p152) the seeds do not contain hydrocyanic acid.

TYPICAL FEATURES
The ve... ... e under-side o... ... have a light cov... ...g of hairs and there are two red pores on the leaf stems.

Step 1: COMPARE WITH THE MAIN PICTURE

Each main picture illustrates the species in its natural habitat, showing the complete tree or shrub or its distinguishing features. Easily confused species are often shown on the same page.

Step 2: IDENTIFICATION OF DISTINGUISHING FEATURES

The two illustrations and additional photograph clearly indicate the distinguishing features and provide useful additional information for identification. Using these pictures will enable you to identify species with certainty.

Step 3: IDENTIFICATION TEXT

The identification text uses clear and simple language to describe important classification features of trees and shrubs, including detailed indications of size. In addition, there is information about a plant's native habitat, explaining where a species of tree or shrub can be found, further general information and descriptions of similar species. This is often a great help in identification.

Step 4: CALENDAR CLOCK

Light-grey segments indicate the flowering period of the tree or shrub, and dark grey indicates the months in which fully ripened fruit can be found hanging from the branches. If there is a period during which the woody plant is both flowering and fruiting, this is indicated in both colours. Climate, weather conditions and habitat can produce variations, of course.

In bloom
In fruit

Step 5: INFOBOX

The coloured Infobox provides useful additional information. In combination, these steps can help you to identify a species with accuracy.

TYPICAL FEATURES

The veins on the underside of the leaf have a light covering of hairs, and there are red pores on the leaf stems.

Trees
and Shrubs

> The trunk of the Sycamore divides into several main branches relatively close to the ground.

The fascinating world of trees and shrubs

Trees and shrubs come in a huge variety of shapes and sizes, but all have one element in common: they are all made of wood. Trees and shrubs can be grouped together under the classification of woody plants. Wood is a hard and durable material, which provides woody plants with stability and enables them to survive through the harshest winters.

A variety of shapes and sizes

The wooden skeleton of a tree consists of a trunk, from which the main branches grow, and a crown of thinner branches and twigs. The newest twigs are called shoots. Many trees, both conifer-ous and deciduous, have stalk-like shoots in addition to the longer branches. These small, side-shoots

> The Juniper always grows to form a narrow, columnar shape.

8

do not grow long but carry the leaves or blossom.

Like trees, shrubs consist of branches and twigs which, depending on the species, form a loose or densely packed crown. Some shrubs, such as the Scotch Broom, form rod-like branches. These grow almost perfectly straight, very rarely branching, but bending slightly outwards.

Large or small

Each woody plant has a maximum adult height. In dwarf shrubs like the Common Heather, this can be less than one metre. Several European species of coniferous and deciduous trees

> The winter, bare branches of the Common Beech.

can reach a height of 30 metres or more. In nutrient-poor habitats, such as moorland or mountainous regions, there are shrubs that grow very close to the ground. Examples of these are Bog Bilberry or Common Bearberry, which grow like creepers along the ground. Some woody plants are also climbers, with branches specially equipped to enable the plant to climb upwards. The maximum height achieved by these species is mainly dependent on the structure used for support.

> The Sloe is a typical shrub with branches that divide several times just above the ground.

> Mistletoe is a shrub that lives in the branches of other trees.

LATIN NAMES

Each species of tree and shrub has a Latin or scientific name in addition to its English name. These names are the same internationally. The first part of the name indicates the genus, eg. *Salix* for willows, and the second part indicates the species, eg. *Salix alba* for the White Willow.

9

> In autumn, the veins of the Japanese Maple leaf are clearly visible.

The leaves of woody plants

Leaves are the power-stations of woody plants. They use sunlight to produce all of the food necessary for growth. Trees and shrubs that retain their leaves all year round are called evergreens. Pine trees and Holly are typical examples of evergreen plants. Even evergreen leaves have a definitive lifespan, however, and are constantly being renewed according to a specific cycle. Some deciduous trees retain their leaves in winter, and only produce new leaves in spring. Most European trees are deciduous. This means that they only have leaves during the warmer part of the year. New leaves appear in spring, having survived the cold winter protected inside buds. With the onset of warmer weather, these buds burst open and the leaves unfold and begin to grow. Fresh leaves normally bear all of the distinguishing features of fully-developed leaves but are glossier and paler in colour.

The colours of autumn

Deciduous woody plants loose their leaves in the autumn. Only by doing so can they survive the cold and lack of usable moisture of the winter season. This loss of leaves nevertheless represents an enormous decrease in biomass. For this reason, in late summer, woody plants begin transferring their valuable chlorophyll and its by-products from the leaves into special storage tissues. The pigments that remain in the leaves give trees their wonderful autumn colouring.

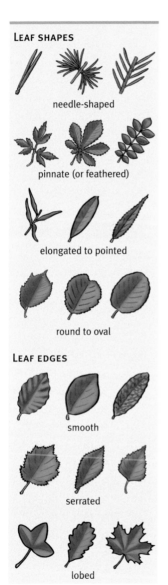

LEAF SHAPES

needle-shaped

pinnate (or feathered)

elongated to pointed

round to oval

LEAF EDGES

smooth

serrated

lobed

Leaves used as identifiers

In many woody plants, the blossoms and fruits can be hard to spot and recognise. As a result, leaves can prove to be useful in identifying trees and shrubs. Leaves are a particularly important identification tool, because they can be found on the tree even when it is not in bloom or in fruit. The shape of the leaves, the patterning on the leaf surface and the arrangement of leaves on twigs all vary from species to species.

Leaf arrangement

Leaf arrangement means the way in which the leaves are positioned on the branches and twigs. If two leaves are always positioned facing each other, then this is an opposite arrangement. If several leaves stem from the same point, this is called a whorl. Alternating leaves are found singly, staggered along the length of a twig.

The anatomy of the leaf

Leaves are normally found on the end of a short stem extending from a branch, but this stem is not always present. Small leaves, sprouting directly where the branch joins the stem are called stipules. At the end of the leaf stem is the leaf face or blade. The stem extends down the centre of the leaf face, forming a central vein. Other, smaller veins extend from this central vein towards the leaf edges.

11

> Common Ash

Shapes of woody plants

Saplings and shrubs often have no definite shape or form, and it is hard to distinguish between individual species. Characteristic tree shapes normally emerge only in the adult tree.

A variety of shapes

The crown of the deciduous tree comes in a variety of shapes, from the spherical crown of the Ash to the irregular shape of the Common Oak. The shape of the crown is determined by the number and arrangement of the main branches.

Conifers have a narrow, columnar shape, and the branches are arranged evenly around a vertical trunk.

The arrangement of the branches can also help to identify the species. For example, the Silver Birch has distinctive hanging branches, while the Scotch Broom has rod-shaped branches.

> Silver Birch

> Common Heather

12

> Common Juniper

> Silver Fir

> Common Elderberry

> Scotch Broom

> Ivy growing on a Common Oak

> Common Oak

13

> Apple blossoms attract many pollinating insects.

Woody plants and their blooms

The anatomy of a bloom can best be seen on wild roses or ornamental shrubs. There is an outermost circle of green, leaf-like sepals called the calyx. These form a protective layer around the flower during the bud stage. Next comes the corolla, the arrangement of coloured petals. In the centre of the bloom is the male, pollen-bearing stamen and the female carpel, consisting of a stigma and style. Pollen from the stamens lands on the stigma of other flowers and pollinates it.

It is the purpose of bright flowers to attract insects. These pollinate the flowers and are

> A panicle of umbels on a Mountain Ash

> Catkins hanging from a Birch tree

> Cones on a Nordmann Fir

rewarded with nectar and pollen.

Many trees and shrubs use a different pollination strategy. They do not have impressive flowers but instead produce massive amounts of pollen, which is then carried on the wind to pollinate the blossoms on other trees.

Strength in numbers

Trees and shrubs often have several blooms sprouting from a single flower stem to form a cluster. Often, a woody plant will produce entirely male clusters or entirely female clusters.

Several woody plants form catkins, consisting of barely perceptible individual flowers densely clustered on a single shaft. A raceme is a series of quite large flowers on stalks, arranged in a row along a shaft. If this shaft is branched, it is called a panicle. An umbel is a cluster of individual flowers originating from the same point, but which are all of a similar length, resulting in a flat top. Mixed arrangements are also possible, such as a branched panicle with umbellate clusters.

Cones

In conifers, the reproductive organs of the female are located inside the scaly female cones. When the seeds are fully developed, they fall from the cone and drift to the ground on wing-like structures. The male cones are normally much smaller and produce countless pollen grains.

> Red Horse-Chestnut flowers are arranged in a panicle.

> The Chinese Wisteria forms long racemose clusters.

> The Japanese Rose has individual flowers.

15

> These Spindle Tree capsules are already open.

Woody plants and their fruits

Pollination occurs when the wind or an insect carries pollen from one plant to the stigma of another plant of the same species. The pollen grain then grows a tubular extension to connect with the ovary. The pollen and the egg combine, and the result is a seed containing an embryo.

Depending on the species, the number of seeds developing in the ovary can range from one to many. While the seeds are developing to maturity, the ovary swells to become a fruit.

Expert fliers

Several plants, such as the various

> The Scotch Broom forms pods.

> Blackberries are aggregate fruits.

> Wild Cherries are stone fruits.

species of maple or birch produce seeds with wing-like extensions. These catch the wind and carry the seed over great distances. Willows and Poplar seeds achieve the same results because they are covered with fine, light hairs.

A carnival of colour

Another strategy for seed dispersal is to provide edible fruits for animals. The seeds are not normally digested and are excreted from the animal far from the mother plant. Berries are fleshy fruits which can contain one or several seeds. Stone fruits, or drupes, have a soft outer layer and a hard, woody stone that surrounds and protects the seeds. Nuts, on the other hand, consist only of a hard, external shell. In some species, the shell of the fruit dries out and only opens when fully ripe, thus releasing the seeds. This is true of pods and capsules. Pods consist of one or two carpels that split along the edge, while capsules consist of multiple carpels.

Aggregate fruits

Aggregate fruits grow together in a cluster or bunch. Examples are blackberries and raspberries. Pomaceous fruits include Apples and Pears, as well as the Quince, Medlar and Hawthorn. The rose hip is another aggregate fruit, of a type only found on roses.

> Guelder Rose berries

> Hazelnuts are true nuts.

> Crab-apples on a Wild Crab tree.

> Rose hips on a Japanese Rose.

> Pale bark is very typical of the Birch.

Bark, thorns and roots

In addition to the leaves, flowers and fruits of a tree or shrub, it is also helpful to examine the bark, the outer surface of the plant, in order to accurately identify it.

No rose without a thorn?

To be scientifically accurate, a distinction must be made between spines and thorns. Spines are modified leaves, stipules, shoots and sometimes even roots. The Black Locust and the Barberry are typical spiny plants. As for the rose, the pointed excrescences on a rose are true thorns, that is to say, modified and reduced branches.

In individual cases, it is not always easy to distinguish between a spine and a thorn. However, the species descriptions in this book use the terms correctly. Both spines and thorns protect the plant against being eaten.

Trees and their 'skin'

Very young shoots, as well as leaves and fruits, are covered by a thin layer of living cells. This 'skin' is sometimes also covered in individual or densely packed hairs, and it is often different in colour to older branches. Fruits are also sometimes covered in a waterproof, waxy layer, giving the surface a polished appearance. Within a year, new shoots develop a new skin, called the bark. This consists of lignified cells, i.e. cells that have turned into wood and have died. The bark can be smooth or may have bumps and cracks, as in the Field Maple or Small-leaved Elm.

In some trees and shrubs, such as the Hornbeam, the growth of the bark matches the growth of the trunk circumference, and this external layer continues to be formed throughout the life of the tree. Usually, however, the bark is a more rigid structure, and as the trunk thickens, the bark cracks. In order to safely protect the trunk, trees often produce new, deep layers of corky cells. The oldest layers of bark then fall off in small or large flakes. Although there are various names for the different layers of tree bark, this book only uses the general term 'bark' for the sake of clarity. The structure and colour of the bark are characteristics that can help identify tree and shrub species.

Above and below the ground

The roots of a tree firmly anchor the trunk and the crown in the earth. They extract water and nutrients in the soil that are needed by the plant for growth. Some species form roots above ground. Ivy, for example, uses anchoring roots in order to enable it to climb up a supporting structure. The roots emerge directly from the branches and work their way into the smallest cracks and crevices.

> The Common Barberry bears long, sharp spines.

> The sharp projections on roses are true thorns.

> Most Holly leaves have sharp, pointed spikes.

> Ivy climbs using its powerful anchoring roots.

The annual cycle of woody plants

Evergreen conifers look pretty much the same year round, apart from when they produce flowers. The majority of deciduous trees and shrubs, however, change significantly in appearance depending on the season.

Before the start of spring

As the days begin to lengthen and the temperature rises, growth inhibitors begin to leave the dormant buds. Cells in the growing tissues resume their activity, and the roots begin to take up water once more after the winter period of dormancy.

Spring

New growth begins in the buds of the previous year. The sturdy coverings or scales expand to make room for tiny new leaves. The same process occurs in the flower buds. In some species of woody plant, the flowers emerge before the leaves. Inside the buds, the leaves and flowers are already fully formed, but minute. They begin to grow and expand until the bud scales split open from the pressure. Within a few days or weeks, the branches will have a completely new covering of greenery, and the leaves will continue to grow until they reach their full size.

Early summer

Most trees and shrubs bloom in early summer. The male plant's reproductive organs produce pollen, which is then carried by the wind or by insects to the female flowers. After pollination, the egg is fertilised by the pollen grain inside the ovary. The ovary ripens into a fruit, in which the seeds and seedlings develop.

Midsummer

Most fruits ripen in midsummer. Each tree and shrub forms its own characteristic fruits, which employ a variety of strategies to ensure that the seeds are carried as far from the mother tree as possible. The food and energy produced by the leaves provide all the growing parts of the tree or shrub with sufficient energy. Any excess is carefully stored away by the plant.

Hazel catkins

Mezereon

Wild Rose

Laburnum flowers

Before spring   **Spring**

WINTER – LIFE ON HOLD

Deciduous tree and shrubs manage to survive winter by entering into a kind of hibernation. The leaves are shed in autumn, and all life-functions are reduced to a minimum. Water is removed from the circulation systems, and all the sensitive growing tissues are protected from the cold by buds. But it is not only the cold that threatens the trees and shrubs. Shortage of water is also a problem. Like hibernating animals, plants must also reduce their metabolism and life-functions to a

complete minimum, and this requires water. The loss of leaves in autumn and the formation of buds are both effective methods of minimising loss of water to the surrounding environment.

Autumn

As an initial preparation for the onset of winter, trees and shrubs begin to empty their leaves of chlorophyll, the valuable substance that enables plants to create energy. As the chlorophyll drains from the leaves, the residual colours in the leaves become visible. Many leaves look yellow due to the chemicals and pigments that they contain naturally, but some trees also produce a red or purplish pigment, creating a wonderfully colourful autumn display. A hot dry summer will produce a more varied and longer-lasting autumn colouration and if the autumn is dry and windless, the leaves will stay longer on the tree before they eventually fall. The tissue connecting the leaf stem to the branch begins to separate from other layers of tissue, and eventually the join becomes so loose that a light wind will carry the leaf away from the tree. The tree is left bare and ready to endure the winter.

Willow seeds

Elderberry fruit

Rose hips

Ivy blooms

Summer | Autumn

Woody plants and their habitat

The United Kingdom only has about 150 native species of tree and shrub. A native species is one that occurs naturally and has not been introduced as an ornamental plant. Each individual species has a particular habitat in which it prefers to grow. The habitat of a plant is dictated by natural, external factors. The most important of these is the length of the growing season. The growing season in the Highlands of Scotland, for instance, where the winter lasts for much longer, is significantly shorter than in sheltered regions further south. The type of soil, chalky, acidic or marshy, also plays an important role in determining whether or not a particular species will flourish.

How it all came to be

The history of the world's climate is cyclical. Warm periods follow cold periods, only to to be followed once more by warmth. The strongest influences on the vegetation of our planet have been the Ice Ages. The last Ice Age ended about 10,000 years ago. At that time, the climate of most of Europe was like that of the Arctic tundra of today.

As the climate began to warm up again, and the ice retreated northwards and to the high mountains, warmth-loving plants began to move into new habitats.

MOUNTAIN FORESTS

Only specially adapted species of woody plants can survive in the highest mountainous wooded areas. They grow very slowly, normally only reaching the size of a shrub, since they have to survive long, cold, snowy winters. The tree line marks the areas above which only herbaceous plants and dwarf shrubs can grow.

ORCHARD MEADOWS

Orchards are an ancient form of fruit cultivation. They were not just used for intensive fruit-growing; other crops were also grown among the trees. Today, they represent an important cultural heritage and many unusual fruit varieties can only be found there.

Gradually, the landscape and the typical habitats that we know today came into being.

Man's effect on the landscape

Without humans, the whole of the British Isles would be covered in dense forest. Since the Stone Age, but mainly since the Middle Ages, humans have had a great impact on the natural landscape. They have cut down forests to make room for settlements and agriculture, and pushed numerous species of trees and shrubs back into the remaining unspoilt natural habitats. Natural habitat has turned into cultivated landscape. In so doing, humans have created new environments. Intensive livestock farming and regular deforestation have created heathland, with its dwarf shrubs and birches. Hedgerows dividing fields have provided many shrubs with a new type of habitat.

New plants, new habitat

The desire for ornamental trees or shrubs laden with blossom has led to a constant influx of exotic plants into the United Kingdom. Many of these ornamentals did not survive this transition into our parks and gardens, but other species have coped very well with our climate. They have become wild and have spread naturally throughout their new habitat. The Butterfly Bush and trees such as Walnut and Red Horse-Chestnut are examples of introduced species.

WOODLAND EDGES

Woodland edges are a particularly rich habitat. More light can penetrate here than in the centre of a forest, and plants bask in the sunlight, rather than being over-shadowed by the tree canopy. Woodland edges, like the few remaining coppices and copses, are home to a particularly large variety of woody plants.

HEDGEROWS

Originally, hedgerows were planted by farmers to divide their fields, and protect them from the wind. Today, they are a haven and a shelter for many native species of shrub, and they also provide habitats for countless small creatures, including mammals.

List of trees and shrubs

Common Heather
Scotch Heather
Calluna vulgaris

DESCRIPTION: Common Heather is an evergreen plant, 20–50cm high. It rarely grows as an individual bush but rather covers large areas ①. Its horizontal or vertical branches frequently divide to form further branches.

LEAVES: The minute, hard leaves are arranged in four rows along the length of the branch and are overlapping ③.

BLOOMS: The blooms are pink, and sometimes white, and form dense racemes ②. Each individual flower consists of four identical sepals and four shorter but similar petals ④.

TYPICAL FEATURES
The low-growing shape of Common Heather and its four true petals make the plant very easy to identify.

FRUITS: The spherical capsule fruits are only a few millimetres long.

DISTRIBUTION: On nutrient-poor, acidic soil; in light pine woodland, heathland, moorland and dunes.

OTHER: The stiff but flexible branches used to be made into brooms.

Common Crowberry
Black Crowberry
Empetrum nigrum

DESCRIPTION: The evergreen Crowberry forms a dense covering, 10–30cm high ①. Its branches lie mainly horizontally, or are raised only very slightly upwards. The newest shoots are often reddish in colour.

LEAVES: The leathery, stiff and somewhat fleshy leaves are arranged around the branches ②. Their edges curve down sharply.

BLOOMS: The minute red blooms ③ have three

TYPICAL FEATURES
The Common Crowberry has characteristic small, stiff leaves with a shiny surface.

sepals and petals. Male and female flowers do not grow on the same plant.

FRUITS: The spherical, blue-black fruits ④ are about the size of a pea. They look like berries, but botanically speaking, they are actually stone fruits containing more than one stone.

DISTRIBUTION: On peaty or sandy soil; in dunes, in dry areas on moors; in mountain ranges, though not in the Alps.

OTHER: The leaves are alkaloid, but the fruits are harmless to eat – they are rather bland and flavourless, however.

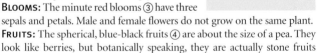

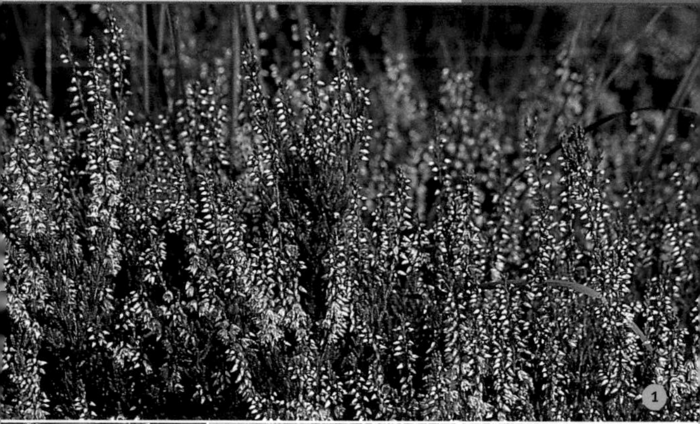
1

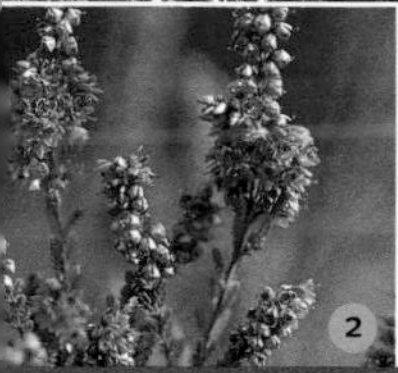
2

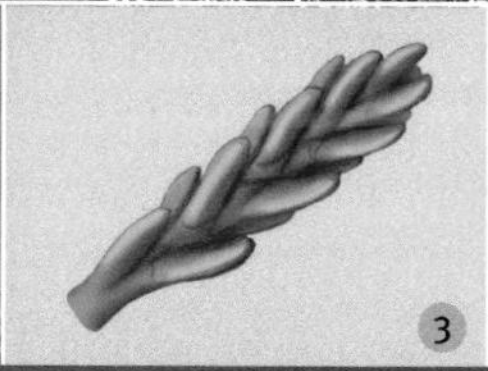
3

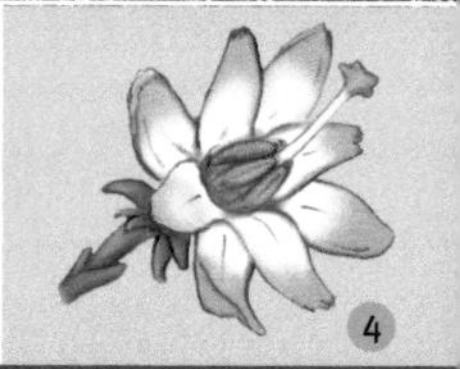
4

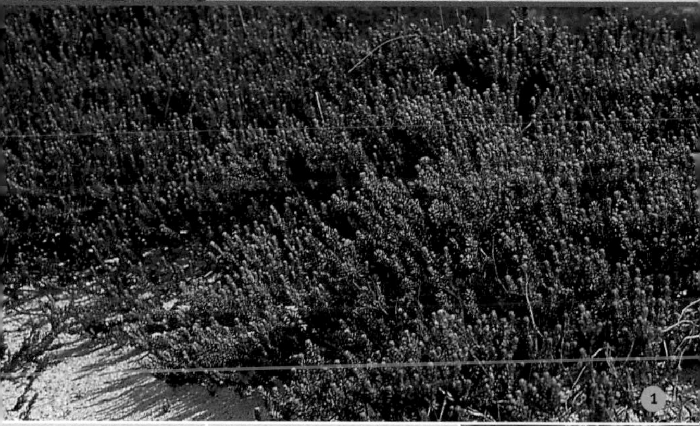
1

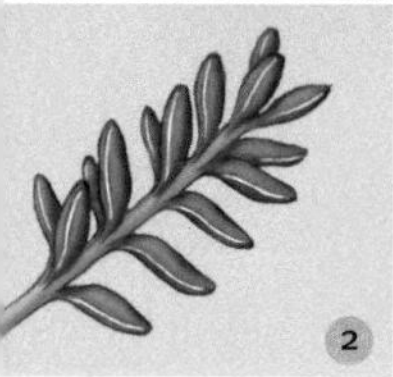
2

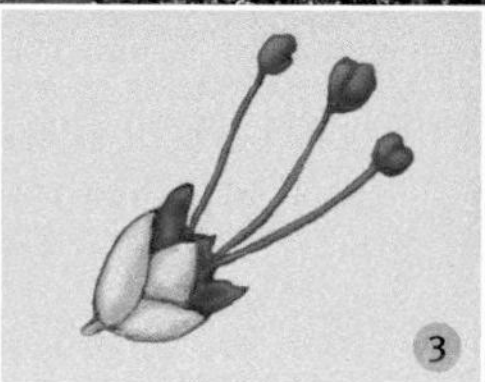
3

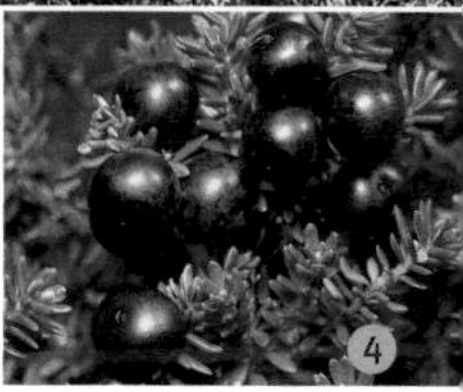
4

Cross-leaved Heath

Bog Heather

Erica tetralix

DESCRIPTION: A low evergreen shrub, which grows horizontally along the ground, only reaching a height of 20–60cm. Flower-bearing shoots ① grow vertically. The plant always has noticeable hairs, which can be very dense.

LEAVES: Hairy leaves never more than 1cm long ③ arranged in fours in a whorl, almost at right angles to the branch ④.

BLOOMS: Light pink flowers clustered at the ends of branches. They hang from a short stem which bends slightly forward. Its petals grow to form a bulbous tube, ending in four curved lips ②. The stamen rarely extends past the petals.

FRUITS: When the inconspicuous capsule fruits are ripe, they remain enclosed within the flower, but this changes to a rust-red colour.

DISTRIBUTION: Requires boggy, nutrient-poor soil in peat or sand; heathland and moors; normally in lowland areas.

TYPICAL FEATURES

Cross-leaved Heath can be identified by its leaves, arranged in groups of four, and by its slightly hairy sepals and bud scales.

Winter Heath

Erica carnea

DESCRIPTION: An evergreen dwarf shrub, only 25cm high. Forms dense branches that provide extensive ground cover. Young, thin branches are very flexible and angular; older branches become woody and dark-brown.

LEAVES: The short leaves are needle-shaped but soft ②, and arranged in fours in a whorl. In winter they change colour from a dark green to a muddy green.

BLOOMS: The light to dark pink flowers ④ are arranged close together in large numbers at the end of the branches, all facing in the same direction. The petals grow into a deep cup shape.

TYPICAL FEATURES

Winter Heath is the earliest flowering species of heather, hence its name ①.

FRUITS: The capsule fruits remain surrounded by the petals ③.

DISTRIBUTION: In chalky, loose and stony soil; in light coniferous woods and the foothills of the Alps.

OTHER: The flower buds form as early as late summer and lie dormant until they bloom the following spring.

29

Common Juniper
Juniperus communis

DESCRIPTION: The evergreen Common Juniper branches very close to the ground and has several main branches which can grow to a height of 10m. It is most commonly found as a small bush. Branches grow vertically and form a tapering, columnar crown ①.

LEAVES: The needle-like leaves are arranged in whorls of three ②. They are hard and sharp and end in a fierce point.

TYPICAL FEATURES
The Juniper can be easily identified by its groups of three needles and its blue-black fruits.

BLOOMS: The male flowers ③ are yellow, and the female flowers form green cones about 2mm long. Both grow where the needle joins the branch, normally on different plants.

FRUITS: The juniper berries ④ develop from the cone and are initially green. They remain on the shrub for 2–3 years, until they are fully developed. Only then do they take on their characteristic blue-black colouring.

DISTRIBUTION: In nutrient-poor soil; in light pine woodland, dry slopes and on heathland.

Common Yew
Taxus baccata

DESCRIPTION: The Yew is an evergreen shrub that can reach 15m in height and has a rough trunk that normally branches near to the ground. The shape of the crown can vary from narrow and tapered to almost round ①. On older plants, the red-brown bark flakes away in large pieces ②.

LEAVES: On the young, horizontal branches, the flat, needle-like leaves are arranged in two rows. Older branches have needles all around.

TYPICAL FEATURES
Since the Yew can come in a variety of shapes and forms, the unique berry is the most useful feature for identification.

BLOOMS: Male and female flowers grow on different plants. Male flowers are spherical and yellow ③ and located on the underside of the branches. The female flowers look like tiny green buds.

FRUITS: The individual, blue-black seeds are surrounded by a fleshy, bright red berry when fully developed ④.

DISTRIBUTION: In shady mixed and beech woodland, but most frequently found growing as an ornamental in churchyards.

OTHER: With the exception of the berry, all parts of the Yew are poisonous.

Silver Fir

Abies alba

DESCRIPTION: The Silver Fir is evergreen and can grow to a height of 50m ①. Saplings have a narrow, tapered crown, but on older trees the crown is more columnar and almost flat at the top. The silver-grey bark is thinly cracked ②.

LEAVES: Needles arranged individually on the branches. There are two white stripes on the underside of the leaf. Needles grow on all sides of young branches, but on sheltered branches they normally grow in two rows.

BLOOMS: The male flowers are 2–3cm long and yellow; the female flower forms green, vertical, cone-shaped clusters, about 2–6cm long.

CONES: The 10–15cm-tall cones stand vertically on the branches ③, even in the treetop.

DISTRIBUTION: In damp soil; in mountainous regions at an altitude of 400–1,600m; often grows in clumps.

TYPICAL FEATURES
The cone scales of the Silver Fir fall off when they are mature, leaving behind an empty cone skeleton on the tree ④.

Nordmann Fir

Abies nordmanniana

DESCRIPTION: The evergreen Nordmann Fir can reach a height of 60m, but is normally only 30m high. Saplings have a pointed, tapering crown ①, that becomes more rounded and columnar with age. The bark is dark-grey with torn flakes.

LEAVES: The needles have a wide leaf base and are arranged on all sides of the branch. They are dark-green and and have two lengthways, white stripes on the underside.

BLOOMS: The spherical, red-coloured male flowers ④ form in dense clusters on the underside of the branches. Female flowers are light green and egg-shaped and are normally found in the treetops. The egg-shaped to spherical buds ② secrete no resin.

CONES: The 15–20cm-long cones stand upright on the branches ③.

DISTRIBUTION: Native to eastern and south-eastern Europe. Grown in the United Kingdom as an ornamental and for Christmas trees.

TYPICAL FEATURES
Unlike the vertical branches of the Silver Fir, the branches of the Nordmann fir grow horizontally and not upwards.

33

Norway Spruce

Picea abies

DESCRIPTION: The evergreen Norway Spruce can grow to a height of 50m and has a very straight, cone-shaped crown ①. Its branches hang slightly downwards. The grey or red-brown bark flakes off in small, thin pieces ②.

LEAVES: The needles are arranged individually on all sides of the branch and are mounted on small pegs.

BLOOMS: The male clusters are up to 3cm long ③ and initially red, then yellow. Male flowers can be found throughout the entire crown, but the reddish female flowers are only found at the top of the tree.

TYPICAL FEATURES
The very hard, stiff needles of the Norway Spruce are 1–2cm long and have four distinct corners in cross-section. Branches without needles have a very rough surface.

CONES: The 10–16cm-long cones hang from the smaller branches ④. Unlike fir cones, they fall from the tree in one piece when they are mature.

DISTRIBUTION: In deep, damp and loose clay soil in mountainous regions and in northern Europe. Popular as a large, outdoor Christmas tree.

Serbian Spruce

Picea omorica

DESCRIPTION: The evergreen Serbian Spruce can reach a height of up to 35m. Its crown is tapered, even in adult trees. The tree can be cone-shaped or pillar-shaped, and its branches begin almost at ground level ①.

LEAVES: The densely arranged needles ④ grow individually from stem-like pegs on all sides of the branch; on sheltered inner branches, needles often grow in two rows.

BLOOMS: Small, male cones are light red and about 1–2cm long; female cones ② are slightly longer, purple-red and stand vertically.

TYPICAL FEATURES
The needles of the Serbian Spruce have two lengthways white stripes on the underside, which make it easy to distinguish from the Norway Spruce.

CONES: The cones are only 4–6cm long and hang from the branch ③; they are initially dark violet, but become brown when mature. They remain on the tree until the following spring.

DISTRIBUTION: Native to mountainous regions of Bosnia and Herzegovina; found as an ornamental conifer throughout Europe; very adaptable plant that will grow well on nutrient-poor soil.

35

Douglas Fir
Pseudotsuga menziesii

DESCRIPTION: Evergreen conifer that can grow up to 50m tall ①. Crown is long, narrow and tapered. In older trees, the shape becomes flatter, and the horizontal branches give the tree an irregular appearance. Bark ② is initially grey, but turns red-brown and smooth.
LEAVES: The relatively soft needles are arranged around the branch or in two rows. The undersides of the needles have two silvery white stripes along the length.

TYPICAL FEATURES
If you crush the needles of a Douglas Fir between your fingers, you will smell a fruity, orange scent.

BLOOMS: Male flowers are yellow and cylindrical, and located on the underside of the branches; female flowers form in vertical green or red, cone-like clusters; buds ③ are spindle-shaped and pointed.
CONES: The 5–10cm-long, hanging cones ④ have rounded scales which extend beyond the three-pointed protective scales.
DISTRIBUTION: Native to the Pacific coast of North America; grown as a park and garden conifer in Europe.

Canadian Hemlock
Tsuga canadensis

DESCRIPTION: The evergreen Canadian Hemlock grows to a height of 20–30m ①. Its crown can be very broad and irregular and the lower branches can stick out very far. The bark is grey-brown and lightly furrowed ②.
LEAVES: Needles are both large and small and are arranged in two rows on tiny stems on the smaller branches ④.
BLOOMS: The male flowers are spherical, yellow-green and only 3mm long. They are located where the needles join the branch. The cone-like, light green female clusters stand vertically on the branches.

TYPICAL FEATURES
The Canadian Hemlock can be identified by the needles, which come in several sizes and are arranged in rows on the branches, and the cones, which are egg-shaped.

CONES: The cones are only about 2cm long ③ and hang in large numbers from the branches. They develop to maturity in the same year in which they are fertilised, but fall to the ground whole in the second year.
DISTRIBUTION: Native to western parts of North America; a common ornamental tree in Central Europe, in damp soil.

37

Giant Sequoia
Sequoiadendron giganteum

DESCRIPTION: The evergreen Giant Sequoia can reach a height of up to 50m in Central Europe ①. The thick, straight trunk carries strong branches, which form a narrow, tapering crown, with gaps. The red-brown bark ② has deep furrows with soft flakes.

LEAVES: The needles ④ are arranged on all sides of the branches. They are scale-like, small and pointed and very narrowly angled away from the branch.

TYPICAL FEATURES
On taller trees, both needles and cones grow too high up for examination, but the Giant Sequoia's thick, straight trunk makes it easily identifiable.

BLOOMS: Male flowers appear in winter and turn yellow in spring. At the same time, the green, cone-like female flower clusters open up.

CONES: In the first year, the egg-shaped, finger-length cones are green, but they turn red-brown in the second year ③.

DISTRIBUTION: Originally from California. Cultivated in Europe, since the nineteenth century, as an ornamental. Prefers damp, nutrient-rich soil.

Dawn Redwood
Metasequoia glyptostroboides

DESCRIPTION: The Dawn Redwood is deciduous and can grow up to 30m tall ①. Its crown is columnar. Juvenile branches grow vertically, but older branches grow outwards or hang slightly down. The bark ② is red-brown and flakes off in stringy pieces.

LEAVES: Flat, soft needles ③ are arranged in two rows on small branches growing either side of a larger branch. In autumn, they turn a variety of red shades ④, and the small

TYPICAL FEATURES
Below where the branches join the trunk, the Dawn Redwood has groove-like cuts in the bark ②.

branches fall off in one piece. Needles on larger branches drop individually.

BLOOMS: The catkin-like male flowers are normally found in the treetops and are 5–10cm long, hanging limply from the branches; female flowers are located at the branch tips in small, green, cone-like clusters.

CONES: The cones are initially green and grow vertically. Mature cones reach a length of 2.5cm, are brown and hang down.

DISTRIBUTION: Native to the Chinese province of Hupeh; grown in parks in Europe.

39

Swiss Stone Pine

Pinus cembra

DESCRIPTION: The evergreen Swiss Stone Pine can reach a height of up to 25m ①. In juvenile trees, the crown is regular and tapered, but with age it becomes irregular. The young branches are green and carry hairs.

LEAVES: The needles are 5–12cm long and grown close to the branch. They are stiff, have a triangular cross-section and grow in groups of five from short branches ③.

BLOOMS: The male flowers ④ normally form at the base of long, young branches. They are egg-shaped with a yellow or red colour. The cone-shaped, violet female clusters stand vertically on young branch tips.

TYPICAL FEATURES
The Swiss Stone Pine differs from other Alpine conifers due to its bushy groupings of five needles; it is therefore easy to identify.

CONES: 5–10cm long, violet-brown, with wide scales ②; cones turn brown after 1–2 years and fall from the tree whole.

DISTRIBUTION: Central Alps and Carpathian Mountains; at an altitude of between 1,400 and 2,700m.

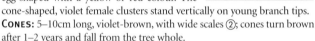

Dwarf Mountain Pine

Mugo Pine

Pinus mugo

DESCRIPTION: The evergreen Dwarf Mountain Pine can grow to form a 25m-tall tree with a spherical crown, or remain a bushy shrub ①. Its bark has grey and black patches.

LEAVES: The needles are always arranged close together in pairs on short branches ②. They are stiff, up to 8cm long, and have a blunt point and a semi-circular cross-section.

BLOOMS: The yellow, male flowers ③ are tightly arranged at the base; the cone-like, red female clusters are located on the tips of young branches.

TYPICAL FEATURES
The cones are about 6cm long and when open are about the same width. They often have an asymmetrical base.

CONES: In autumn of the following year, the cones ④ are bright brown and mature. They form in groups on the branch tips.

DISTRIBUTION: In high mountains at an altitude of about 2,400m; also on moorland and other damp areas. Grown in the United Kingdom as an ornamental.

41

Austrian Pine
Pinus nigra

DESCRIPTION: The evergreen Austrian Pine can reach 30m, and sometimes even 50m tall ①. Saplings have a tapering crown. Branches on older trees grow horizontally and form a flatter, irregular crown.

LEAVES: The needles are arranged in pairs on short twigs. They are very stiff, with a sharp point, and can be up to 15cm long.

BLOOMS: Male flowers are spindle-shaped and yellow ② and form at the base of long twigs. Reddish, cone-like female clusters develop from sharp-pointed buds ③ at ends of small branches and stand vertically.

TYPICAL FEATURES
On older trees, the bark of the Austrian Pine is grey or black with wide cracks ④; this makes it easy to identify.

CONES: Dark-brown, about 10cm long, egg-shaped; develop in groups; when mature, the scales separate widely.

DISTRIBUTION: In the mountains of southern Europe but introduced elsewhere in Europe as a park and garden tree.

Scots Pine | Scotch Pine
Pinus sylvestris

DESCRIPTION: The Scots Pine is an evergreen tree that can reach a height of 40m ①. The crown of juvenile trees is usually tapered, but in older trees this becomes wider and the branches are more loosely arranged. Young branches are yellow-green and without hairs.

LEAVES: The needles are up to 8cm long ④ and are always arranged in pairs on small twig-like branches. They are stiff and often twisted.

BLOOMS: The spindle-shaped, yellow male flowers form close to the base of the newest branches. The cone-shaped female clusters are dark-red to violet and form on the branch tips.

TYPICAL FEATURES
If you have a pair of binoculars, take a look at the trunk at the top of the Scots Pine. The bark is covered in fine scales which have a noticeable reddish colour ③.

CONES: The cones ② take until the following autumn to mature. They are about 8cm long, and roughly egg-shaped with a slight point; they are light brown in colour.

DISTRIBUTION: In Central and Northern Europe, Asia Minor and Siberia; often in sandy soil.

Atlas Cedar
Cedrus atlantica

DESCRIPTION: Evergreen reaching 30–40m in height ①. In saplings, the crown tapers but widens and becomes irregular in older trees, when gaps often appear between the upward-growing branches. Only the crown, where the branches continue to grow straight, remains pointed. Bark is grey-brown with fine cracks.
LEAVES: On larger branches, the needles grow individually on all sides; on twig-like branches, they grow in groups of up to 40 needles ②.
BLOOMS: The yellow male flowers ③ form in large numbers and are up to 6cm long. Female flowers are 1cm long and light green to red in colour.
CONES: The spindle-shaped cones with flattened ends do not mature until the third year. They disintegrate on the branch but the skeletons remain on the tree for years.
DISTRIBUTION: Atlas mountains and as an ornamental in Europe.

TYPICAL FEATURES
The grouped needle arrangement and late blooming period are both characteristics of the Atlas Cedar. The numerous male flowers can be clearly seen.

Weymouth Pine
Eastern White Pine
Pinus strobus

DESCRIPTION: Evergreen ornamental tree in Central Europe, growing to a height of 25m ①. Juveniles have a narrow, tapering crown; branches on older trees grow horizontally in a looser arrangement and turn up slightly.
LEAVES: 15cm-long needles arranged in groups of five ②, loosely distributed along the smaller branches. They are soft and flexible and have a triangular cross-section.
BLOOMS: The male flowers ③ are normally located at the base of new branches. They are just under 1cm long, narrow and yellow. The green, female, cone-like clusters form at the end of the smaller branches.
CONES: In the autumn of the second year, the cones ④ are fully mature. They are up to 20cm long, brown and hang underneath the branches.
DISTRIBUTION: East of North America; Central European parks and woods.
OTHER: In their native habitat these pines can grow to 80m.

TYPICAL FEATURES
The Swiss Stone Pine (p40) also has groups of five needles, but these are much longer on the Weymouth Pine, making it easy to identify.

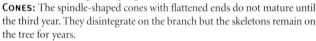

45

European Larch
Larix decidua

DESCRIPTION: The European Larch is a deciduous tree that can grow to a height of 40m ①. The narrow, tapered crown becomes broader and flatter with age.

LEAVES: Large branches are covered in individual flat and soft needles. Small branches have needles in groups of between 20 and 40 ②. Needles have bright green colour in spring, but in autumn they become a rich yellow ④.

TYPICAL FEATURES
On the European Larch, the smaller side-branches hang down from the horizontal main branches.

BLOOMS: Appear just before or at the same time as the needles; the male flowers are yellow and a flat, disc shape, arranged on the underside of the branches; the female clusters are bright red and cone-like and stand vertically on the branches.

CONES: Egg-shaped, brown, 3–4cm long ③; mature by the first autumn, but remain for several years on tree and then fall to ground with the branch.

DISTRIBUTION: Native to mountainous regions of Europe up to the tree line; also grown for timber.

Japanese Larch
Larix kaempferi

DESCRIPTION: A deciduous tree that can grow to a height of 40m. It has a vertical trunk and a broad, tapering crown ①. Its branches grow out horizontally from the trunk. Very young branches are slightly curved. The bark ② quickly turns grey-brown and develops scales.

LEAVES: Larger branches covered in individual, soft, pointed needles; smaller side branches carry groups of between 30 and 40 needles. Autumn colouring is an intense golden yellow.

TYPICAL FEATURES
Unlike the European Larch, young branches on the Japanese Larch never hang down from the main branches.

BLOOMS: Appear just before or at the same time as needles appear on side branches; male flowers are yellow and spherical and located on the underside of branches ④; female flowers form in cone-like clusters ④ which range in colour from green to pink or red and stand vertically on branch tips.

CONES: The oval cones are dark brown ③ and about 4–6cm long. The edges of the scales curve outwards.

DISTRIBUTION: Originates in the Japanese mountains; in Europe is it grown as an ornamental park and garden tree, mainly on the coast.

47

Sabina Juniper | Savin Juniper
Juniperus sabina

DESCRIPTION: The evergreen Sabina Juniper is normally found as a shrub of about 1–2m high ①. Some plants can also grow to form small trees. Its numerous branches grow out in a sidewards direction.

LEAVES: On young shrubs, needle-shaped leaves are arranged in whorls of three. On older shrubs, leaves are arranged in four rows, close to the branch; they look like scales ④.

BLOOMS: The male flowers are only a few millimetres long ③ and are egg-shaped; the female flowers are round, cone-like clusters, which stand vertically on the branches.

TYPICAL FEATURES
If you crush the leaves of the Sabina Juniper between your fingers, they release a very unpleasant smell.

CONES: Berry-like cones mature by first autumn or by the following spring ②. They range in colour from green to blue-black and are bluish when ripe.

DISTRIBUTION: In European high mountain ranges; very rare.

OTHER: All parts of the Sabina Juniper are poisonous.

White Cedar
Thuja occidentalis

DESCRIPTION: The evergreen White Cedar is a tree which can grow to a height of up to 20m. It has a narrow, tapering crown ①. Its dense branches grow upwards. The red-brown, soft bark flakes in long strips from the trunk.

LEAVES: The scale-like leaves lie horizontally, very close to the branch ②, and are arranged in four rows along the length. From above, the leaf-bearing branches are dark green, and from below they appear light green. Crushed leaves smell of herbs.

BLOOMS: The male flowers are yellow-brown and spherical; the female flowers are unremarkable.

TYPICAL FEATURES
The Lawson Cypress (p50) has very similar scale-like leaves, but the White Cedar can be easily distinguished because the branches at the top of the tree always grow vertically.

CONES: Yellow-brown and about 12mm long; initially they are long and narrow ③, but the scales spread widely when the cone is mature ④.

DISTRIBUTION: Eastern North America; in Europe in parks and cemeteries.

OTHER: All parts of the tree are highly poisonous.

49

Lawson Cypress
Chamaecyparis lawsoniana

DESCRIPTION: The Lawson Cypress is an ever-green tree which can grow to a height of 30m. It has a narrow, tapering crown ①. Tips of all branches, including those at the top of the tree, curve down at the ends. The bark is red-brown to silver-brown and flakes off in long strips.

LEAVES: The oval, pointed needles lie against the branches in four, scale-like rows ②. From beneath, the leaves have a whitish edge.

BLOOMS: Form in autumn; male flowers are club-shaped and a bright red colour ③; female flowers are unremarkable and spherical.

CONES: The cones are about 1cm long and are initially blue-green, turning brown later ④; they consist of eight scales, each with a stem.

DISTRIBUTION: North American Pacific coast; ornamental plant in Europe.

OTHER: The Lawson Cypress is poisonous in all its parts.

TYPICAL FEATURES
The Lawson Cypress can be distinguished from the very similar White Cedar (p48) because the branches at the top of the tree always hang down.

Western Red Cedar
Thuja plicata

DESCRIPTION: The evergreen Western Red Cedar can reach a height of 30m ①. It has a tapering crown, becoming steeper at the top. The branches grow out horizontally. The red-brown, soft bark ② flakes off in long strips.

LEAVES: The scale-like needles are only about 3mm long, and lie very close to the branch ④. From above they are a shiny, dark green colour. From below they are grey-green.

BLOOMS: The male flowers are only a few millimetres long and are located on the tips of the branches. The female flower clusters are larger and cone-like, but similarly unremarkable.

TYPICAL FEATURES
The Western Red Cedar can be distinguished from similar species because its crown becomes steeper at the top. It also has a fruity smell and egg-shaped cones.

CONES: Cones are initially green, eventually turning brown. They consist of 10–12 leathery scales which curve sharply outwards ③.

DISTRIBUTION: Pacific North America; grown in Europe as an ornamental in parks and gardens.

OTHER: The Western Red Cedar is poisonous.

Scotch Broom
Cytisus scoparius

DESCRIPTION: The Scotch broom is a deciduous shrub, 1–2m in height ①, with erect rod-like branching stems.

LEAVES: The ternate leaves ② consist of three short haired leaflets, each 1cm long. Simple leaves also grow around the flowers.

BLOOMS: The large, golden yellow flowers ④ have a butterfly-like form: one petal points upwards while two others – the wings – sprout laterally; the two lower petals fuse together to form a keel.

TYPICAL FEATURES

The Scotch Broom often appears rather bare because its leaves can drop early. Its stems have five angular ridges.

FRUITS: The pods ③, 4–5cm in length, start out green then turn black as they ripen. They are densely haired, especially on their edges.

DISTRIBUTION: By waysides and on embankments, in open woodland; in loose, stony or sandy soils.

OTHER: All parts of the Scotch Broom contain poisonous substances.

Gorse
Ulex europaeus

DESCRIPTION: Gorse is an evergreen shrub ①, with extraordinarily dense branches that can grow up to 2m high. The dark green stems carry rigid spines, 2–3cm in length ②, which are branched longitudinally.

LEAVES: When mature, the shrub has no leaves. The chlorophyll is contained in the branches and spines. Only young plants have clover-like ternate leaflets.

TYPICAL FEATURES

The dense spiny Gorse branches are green and grooved along their length.

BLOOMS: The yellow flowers ④ appear in pairs or individually where the scale-like leaflets join the branch, mainly at the ends of the branches. They consist of a keel formed from two fused petals, an erect standard and two wings.

FRUITS: The 2cm-long pods ③ are densely covered all over in hair.

DISTRIBUTION: On coastal heathland throughout the United Kingdom and the rest of Western Europe, and in sandy to stony soils.

OTHER: All parts of Gorse are poisonous.

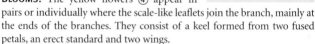

Stone Bramble
Rubus saxatilis

DESCRIPTION: The deciduous Stone Bramble is a shrub that grows to only 25cm in height. The stems are not woody and have fine prickles ④. While the flowerless growth sprawls untidily outwards, its flowering parts are erect.

LEAVES: The long-stemmed leaves are pinnate. They consist of three nearly-oval leaflets, whose edges are irregularly serrated ②.

BLOOMS: The greenish-white flowers form an umbellate cluster. The five petals are very narrow and the sepals bend backwards after flowering ③.

TYPICAL FEATURES
The surest sign of the Stone Bramble is its pea-sized red berry, which remains separate and does not form a compound fruit.

FRUITS: When ripe, the red fruits, which are about the size of peas, form loose clusters of between two and six fruits ①.

DISTRIBUTION: In deciduous and open mixed coniferous forests; in loose soils in partial shade.

Oregon Grape | Holly Grape
Mahonia aquifolium

DESCRIPTION: The Oregon Grape is an evergreen shrub that grows to 50–150cm in height. Its spineless stem has few branches.

LEAVES: Leaves are pinnate and grow very close to the twigs. Each leaflet is edged with fine spines ②. They are leathery and a glossy green, but in winter usually turn red.

BLOOMS: The numerous fragrant golden yellow flowers fuse together in broad upright racemes ④. Each of the flowers, which measure about 1cm across, is hemispherical in shape ③.

TYPICAL FEATURES
The combination of spiny leaves and yellow racemes or, later, dark berries, makes the Oregon Grape an unmistakable plant.

FRUITS: The blue berries ①, which deepen in colour to blue-black when fully ripe, exude a dark red juice when squeezed.

DISTRIBUTION: Native to north-western North America; occurs in Central Europe as an ornamental plant but occasionally also in the wild.

OTHER: The Oregon Grape is mildly poisonous, especially the berries.

Japanese Rose
Rosa rugosa

DESCRIPTION: The deciduous Japanese Rose is a shrub that grows to about 1–5m in height. Its stems, which branch regularly, are densely covered with straight thorns and bristles ②.

LEAVES: Its leaves consist of five to nine leaflets, wrinkled on their upper surface ③ and hairy underneath. Edges are smooth or slightly serrated. At the base of the stalk there are broad sub-leaves with ear-like protrusions. In autumn, the foliage turns brilliant yellow.

BLOOMS: The pink-red, or less commonly white, flowers ① have five shell-like leaves arranged around numerous stamen in the centre of the flower, which measures up to 8cm across.

FRUITS: The bright red hips ④ are compressed to a near spherical shape.

DISTRIBUTION: Native to East Asia; planted in Europe as an ornamental shrub, but also established, especially in coastal regions.

TYPICAL FEATURES
The wrinkled foliage and very densely thorny stems are distinctive features of the Japanese Rose.

Dog Rose
Rosa canina

DESCRIPTION: The Dog Rose is a deciduous shrub that can reach 3m in height ①. When unsupported it has a rounded shape. Branches sometimes put down roots and creep or climb. Stems carry strongly curved thorns.

LEAVES: The pinnate leaves consist of five to seven elliptical serrated leaflets ②. The underside of the leaf is usually covered in silky hair.

BLOOMS: Five-petalled flowers, either solitary or in small clusters ④, grow up to 6cm across on hairless stalks; pale pink to pink in colour, although occasionally also white.

FRUITS: The ovoid hips ③, up to 2.5cm long, turn a deep red when ripe. They are very rich in vitamins and for centuries have been made into tasty syrups, jams and jellies.

DISTRIBUTION: The most common wild rose in Central Europe, found along waysides, in thickets and hedges; also at forest margins.

TYPICAL FEATURES
Typical features of the Dog Rose are its curved thorns and solitary style of the fruit node.

Shrubby Cinquefoil
Golden Hardhack | *Potentilla fruticosa*

DESCRIPTION: The deciduous shrubby cinquefoil is a dense 1m-high shrub ①. Pruned garden specimens, in particular, have numerous branches. Young growth is green and hairy, whilst older wood has a brown bark, which sheds scales.

LEAVES: Leaves are pinnate, ternate or palmate ②, the elongated leaflets grow up to about 1cm in length. Both sides of the leaf are hairy.

BLOOMS: Golden yellow flowers ④ grow very close to the stems. Each flower is surrounded by two rows of five sepals.

FRUIT: Small hairy nuts are enveloped in long brown sepals, even when ripe.

DISTRIBUTION: Native to southern Europe; often planted as an ornamental shrub, but now wild close to human habitation.

TYPICAL FEATURES
The two rows of sepals surrounding the buds are highly distinctive ③; in the outer row they are very narrow, while in the inner row they are broad and triangular.

Raspberry
Rubus idaeus

DESCRIPTION: The Raspberry is a deciduous shrub ① growing 50–150cm in height. Stems are erect and arch over when they grow long. They are round and ribbed and only their lower sections grow thorns, which are barely 1mm in length and coloured deep red ②.

LEAVES: Leaves consist of three, or sometimes up to seven, serrated leaflets whose undersides are covered in a white down.

BLOOMS: The white flowers ③ form erect panicles. Each flower has five petals and five sepals.

TYPICAL FEATURES
As well as its red fruit, the distinctive features of the Raspberry are the downy white undersides of its leaves and dark red thorns.

FRUIT: The raspberry is actually a soft, red cluster of individual, fragile stone fruits with tiny pips. It ripens in late summer ④. The fruit detaches easily from its core and is deliciously edible.

DISTRIBUTION: In open woodland and undergrowth, on embankments and river banks; in nutrient-rich soils; common almost everywhere.

Dewberry
Rubus caesius

DESCRIPTION: The deciduous Dewberry is a climbing shrub that reaches about 1m in height, but also develops creeping shoots. When these take root at their tips, the plant often forms a dense growth ①.

LEAVES: The trefoil pinnate leaves ④ have short hairs on their undersides and irregularly serrated edges. The central leaflet has its own stalk, whereas the two lateral leaflets attach directly to the branch.

TYPICAL FEATURES
The round fruit, bluish when ripe, is covered in fine, straight or curved, needle-like thorns.

BLOOMS: The white flowers ③ have five sepals and five petals and form flattened umbellate displays.

FRUIT: The juicy compound fruit starts out green, ripens to black and later turns blue ②.

DISTRIBUTION: At forest margins, in undergrowth and on riverbanks; in damp to wet ground; widespread up to an altitude of 1,000m.

OTHER: The fruit is edible but lacks flavour.

Blackberry
Rubus fruticosus

DESCRIPTION: The Blackberry is a deciduous shrub that may retain its leaves into the winter. The stems grow up to 2m in length ①.

LEAVES: Long, stalked leaves consist of five leaflets with serrated edges ③. The stalk and central rib are spiny.

TYPICAL FEATURES
The long, hanging stems of the Blackberry are covered with numerous thorns of all sizes ②.

BLOOMS: White flowers with five petals form conical clusters at the ends of the previous year's woody growth.

FRUIT: The tasty berry, which changes colour from red to black as it ripens ④, is a compound fruit formed from individual stone fruits. It is easily detached from its core.

DISTRIBUTION: At waysides, on scrubland, at forest margins and in clearings, in undergrowth and hedgerows; common nearly everywhere.

OTHER: Rich fruiting varieties without thorns have been cultivated for garden planting, most of them from non-European species.

Alpine Clematis
Clematis alpina

DESCRIPTION: The Alpine Clematis is a deciduous climbing shrub which can reach 2–3m in height ①. Its flexible, creeping stems take hold wherever they can or else extend across the ground.

TYPICAL FEATURES
Creeping tendrils and conspicuous flowers are unmistakable features of the Alpine Clematis.

LEAVES: Each of its three, stalked leaflets is in turn sub-divided ②. The long tendril at the leaf extremity twines around other stems and branches, anchoring the plant.

BLOOMS: The flowers, which measure up to 10cm across with their petals fully out, are highly conspicuous ④. They consist of four bright blue or violet sepals. The pollen sacs surround a ring of white stamen.

FRUIT: The silvery clusters of fruit consist of numerous individual fruits with long, soft-haired plumes that assist windborne dispersal ③.

DISTRIBUTION: In mountain forests in the Alps and Carpathians from about 1,200m to 2,400m altitude; in nutrient-poor, stony soils.

Wild Clematis
Old Man's Beard | Traveller's Joy
Clematis vitalba

DESCRIPTION: The Wild Clematis is a deciduous climbing shrub which, in favourable conditions, can grow up to 10m in height. Its creeper-like stems can grow to the thickness of a finger. It sheds its bark in long strips.

TYPICAL FEATURES
The combination of silvery-haired fruit ① with creeper-like climbing stems and flaky bark occurs only in the Wild Clematis.

LEAVES: Its pinnate leaves have five to seven leaflets ② and grow up to 25cm long. Their margins are smooth or coarsely toothed.

BLOOMS: The profusion of narrow yellowish-white fluffy stamens in the white flowers is especially striking ④.

FRUIT: Each flower contains numerous small seeds with extended tail-like styles and silky flight hairs ③. Clusters of fruit remain on the plant throughout the winter.

DISTRIBUTION: On the banks of rivers and streams, in thickets and at forest margins; in wet, nutrient-rich soil.

OTHER: The wild clematis is poisonous; its sap can cause skin irritation.

Stag's Horn Sumach

Rhus typhina

DESCRIPTION: The Stag's Horn Sumach is a deciduous shrub spreading 3–5m in all directions ①, or a small tree. Its young stems are downy and it throws out runners and can develop into a thick bush.

LEAVES: Pinnate leaves ② that grow up to 50cm in length. They consist of long pointed leaflets with coarsely toothed margins. In autumn the foliage turns a deep red ①.

BLOOMS: The yellowish-green, inconspicuous flowers occur packed together in large erect racemes ③.

TYPICAL FEATURES

In the fruiting season, dense rust-red conical fruit clusters make the Stag's Horn Sumach unmistakable ④.

FRUIT: The striking rust-red clusters of fruit ④, which ripen into the autumn, contain minute stone fruits with red hairs.

DISTRIBUTION: Eastern North America; an ornamental or garden species in Central Europe but occasionally wild in dry, stony soil.

OTHER: The leaves and fruit of the Stag's Horn Sumach are poisonous.

Tree of Heaven

Ailanthus altissima

DESCRIPTION: The deciduous Tree of Heaven with its erect branches grows up to 25m in height ①. Its trunk is generally straight and it has an irregularly domed crown. Young wood is reddish-brown and forked.

LEAVES: Pinnate leaves ② that can grow 50cm long or more. They consist of numerous narrow leaflets whose lower portions are finely toothed.

BLOOMS: The minute greenish or white flowers are grouped together in erect panicles up to 25cm in length ③. Male and female flowers are found on different plants.

TYPICAL FEATURES

In autumn, the Tree of Heaven's large distinctive leaves fall without changing colour. They leave a distinct triangular scar on the branch.

FRUIT: Reddish-brown seeds hang from the branches in dense clusters ④. Each individual seed has its own leaf-like wing.

DISTRIBUTION: Native to east Asia; introduced to Europe as an ornamental tree; occasionally found in the wild.

Chinese Wisteria
Wisteria sinensis

DESCRIPTION: The Chinese Wisteria is a deciduous climbing shrub, which can reach a height of up to 10m ①. In comparison with its size, it has rather thin stems, which often grow together to form thick, knotty branches.

LEAVES: The pinnate leaves ②, which grow up to 30cm long, are formed of numerous leaflets distributed along the stalk.

BLOOMS: Butterfly-shaped flowers, ranging in colour from light blue to violet, form hanging racemes ④, which can reach 50cm or more in length.

TYPICAL FEATURES
The large blue racemes appear in spring, often before the leaves. They have a very pleasant fragrance.

FRUIT: Downy pods, 10–15cm in length ③, contain relatively large seeds. In the British climate however, they seldom ripen fully.

DISTRIBUTION: Native to East Asia; used in Central Europe as an ornamental planting on walls and arbours.

OTHER: The fruit, bark and roots of the Chinese Wisteria are poisonous.

Laburnum
Laburnum anagyroides

DESCRIPTION: The Laburnum grows to 3–6m in height as a shrub or a small branching tree ①. Its green bark is very smooth.

LEAVES: Its long pinnate leaves are formed from three leaflets up to 8cm in length ②. Young leaves carry short fine hairs.

BLOOMS: The bright yellow butterfly-like flowers grow up to 2cm across and hang in rich racemes.

TYPICAL FEATURES
The young stems of the Laburnum have a green bark, striped along its length. The branches are densely haired, and white buds ③ emerge through the silky silver-grey mat of hairs.

FRUIT: The flat, light brown pods ④ thicken slightly towards their margins and appear compressed between the seeds.

DISTRIBUTION: On sunlit, rocky slopes, in open woodland, on mountains up to 2,000m altitude; frequently planted as an ornamental garden shrub.

OTHER: The Laburnum is highly poisonous throughout. If eaten, the seeds can be lethal, especially for children.

Black Locust | False Acacia
Robinia pseudoacacia

DESCRIPTION: The Black Locust is a deciduous tree with a roundish, sparse crown growing up to 30m high ①. The trunk forks to form thick branches, often very close to the ground. Its thick grey-brown bark is deeply furrowed ②.

LEAVES: A central stalk, 20–30 cm-long, carries numerous oval leaflets with smooth margins ③. Before it falls in late autumn, the foliage turns yellow.

TYPICAL FEATURES

Very sharp spines develop at the point where the stalks of the leaves sprout from the branches.

BLOOMS: Abundant white flowers form hanging racemes, 10–15cm in length ④, which give off a pleasant fragrance.

FRUIT: Flat, brown pods form in September and October but remain on the tree until well into the winter.

DISTRIBUTION: Native to the Atlantic seaboard of North America; planted here in parks and woods; also thrives in nutrient-poor soil.

OTHER: Although not a native species, bees still love the nectar ('Acacia honey').

Boston Ivy
Parthenocissus tricuspidata

DESCRIPTION: Under the right conditions, the deciduous Boston Ivy can reach 10m in height. It anchors itself by means of adhesive discs on forked tendrils, which occur opposite the leaves ②.

LEAVES: The long-stalked, three-lobed leaf is cordate with coarse, jagged margins. In autumn the foliage turns a vivid red ①.

BLOOMS: The minute inconspicuous flowers are green and form small umbrella-shaped panicles ③.

TYPICAL FEATURES

The Boston Ivy is easily distinguishable from the Virginia Creeper thanks to its three-lobed leaves.

FRUIT: Small berries, dark blue or almost black, with a pronounced ribbed surface, often lie out of sight beneath the foliage.

DISTRIBUTION: Native to the eastern seaboard of North America, the ivy has given its name to the Ivy League colleges; an ornamental in Europe.

SIMILAR SPECIES: The five-leaved Virginia Creeper (*Parthenocissus quinquefolia*) has five-lobed pinnate leaves ④. Autumn foliage turns carmine to purple, with blue-black berries in between.

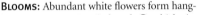

69

Common Elder
Sambucus nigra

DESCRIPTION: The Common Elder is usually a shrub, about 3–7m in height ①. Occasionally, it grows into a small tree with knotty stems. Its light brown bark is pocked with small pores.

LEAVES: Pinnate leaves with long stalks are formed into five to seven leaflets ②, pointed and finely toothed at the margins.

BLOOMS: Small off-white flowers ③ grow in flat topped clusters. They have a powerful fragrance.

TYPICAL FEATURES
The white pith of the stems is a distinctive feature of the Common Elder.

FRUIT: As it ripens, the seeded fruit gradually turns from green to a rich, glossy black ④.

DISTRIBUTION: Widespread; at forest margins, on river and canal banks and in hedgerows.

OTHER: Raw, unripe fruit of the Common Elder can be damaging to health, especially for children. The ripe fruit, on the other hand, can be made into juices, jam and jellies and the flowers are also used to make syrups.

Red Elder
Sambucus racemosa

DESCRIPTION: The deciduous Red Elder is a shrub which grows 1–4m in height; it has erect or hanging stems ① and its branches have a dark brown bark.

LEAVES: Its pinnate foliage grows on long stalks, which can be up to 25cm long, and consists of five to seven leaflets ③. Each is ovoid and pointed and finely serrated at the margin. When crushed or rubbed, the leaves have a powerful and unpleasant smell.

TYPICAL FEATURES
A distinctive feature of the Red Elder outside the fruiting season is the rust-red pith in its hollow stems ②.

BLOOMS: A profusion of small, pale yellow flowers appears simultaneously with the leaves in spring. The flowers form erect conical panicles and are pleasantly fragrant.

FRUIT: Abundant bright red, pea-sized stone fruits, clustering tightly together ④.

DISTRIBUTION: In open woodland and in thickets, as well as by waysides in nutrient-poor, clay soils.

OTHER: The fruit of the Red Elder is mildly poisonous.

Mountain Ash | Rowan
Sorbus aucuparia

DESCRIPTION: The Mountain Ash is a deciduous tree that grows up to 15m in height ①; with its steeply rising branches it can give the appearance of a shrub. Its crown is sparse and ragged.

LEAVES: Pinnate leaves have 9–19 leaflets ②. Each is narrow, pointed and finely serrated at the margin. They turn yellow to red in autumn.

BLOOMS: The small white flowers form broad, flat-topped panicles.

TYPICAL FEATURES
Besides its flowers and fruit, the smooth, almost shiny bark of the Mountain Ash ③ is highly distinctive.

FRUIT: In autumn and sometimes through to winter, the round red fruit hangs in dense clusters ④.

DISTRIBUTION: At forest margins and in clearings, by paths and also as an ornamental plant; widespread as a roadside planting as it is undemanding.

OTHER: The fruit of the Mountain Ash is important in the diet of certain birds. It is rich in vitamins and is likewise edible for humans.

True Service Tree | Whitty Pear
Sorbus domestica

DESCRIPTION: The True Service Tree is a deciduous tree with a rounded crown, growing to about 15m tall or occasionally taller ①. Its young branches are hairy, but as they age they turn bare and cork-like growths form on the bark.

LEAVES: Pinnate leaves consist of up to 21 leaflets. They are narrow and only serrated in their frontal portions. They have a fine down on their undersides. In autumn the foliage turns yellow to red.

TYPICAL FEATURES
The grey-brown bark of the trunk is broken into strips ②. Its fruit also distinguishes it from the Mountain Ash.

BLOOMS: Conical panicles are formed from 6–12 white flowers ③.

FRUIT: Lightly spotted fruit, apple- or pear-shaped with a red blush ④, grow up to 3cm in length.

DISTRIBUTION: Predominantly mixed oak woodland; on calcareous soils; in Central Europe mostly in wine-growing regions with mild climates.

OTHER: The raw fruit is not strictly edible but for many centuries, it has been added to cider to clarify it and improve its keeping properties.

Box Elder
Acer negundo

DESCRIPTION: The Box Elder is a deciduous tree with a sparse, roundish crown growing 15–20m in height ①. It is often found growing with multiple trunks. The young wood is lightly furrowed while the trunk and older branches have a smooth grey-black bark.

LEAVES: Pinnate leaves consist of three or five leaflets ②, the end leaflet itself being trilobed like the maple. Serrations around the leaf margins are coarse and irregular.

BLOOMS: The small, yellowish flowers hang in dense bunches ③, and often appear before the leaves. Male and female flowers occur on different trees.

FRUIT: The seed-bearing fruit turns from green to brown and forms long, hanging bunches ④. The seeds form in two parts, and each wing meets its opposite number at an acute angle or turns slightly inwards.

DISTRIBUTION: North America; planted as an ornamental shrub in Central Europe.

TYPICAL FEATURES
The Box Elder is the only tree with pinnate leaves and maple-like fruit.

Common Ash
Fraxinus excelsior

DESCRIPTION: The Common Ash is a deciduous tree growing up to 40m tall. It has a domed crown whose main branches stand erect ①. The slender trunk has a grey bark with pronounced furrows.

LEAVES: The leaves consist of 9–15 leaflets, which sprout directly from the central stalk ②. Only the terminal leaflet has a stalk of its own. All are ovoid, finely serrated at the margin and downy along their central vein.

BLOOMS: Inconspicuous male and female flowers appear before the leaves in small bushy clusters ③.

FRUIT: Fruit hangs from the branches in dense clusters ④. They are small seed pods with narrow wings which, by contrast with the Maple, whose fruit occurs in pairs, grow singly on a short stalk. When ripe they are light brown.

DISTRIBUTION: In mixed deciduous woodland, forests in lowlands and ravines; in loose soils; frequently planted in parkland or by roadsides.

TYPICAL FEATURES
In winter the Common Ash is distinguished by its plump, blackish-brown buds ③.

Common Walnut

Juglans regia

DESCRIPTION: The deciduous walnut can reach a height of 25m ①. Its trunk branches fairly close to the ground and forms several strong branches.

LEAVES: Leaves are seven to nine ovoid leaflets, smooth at the margins, increasing in size from the base to the terminal leaflet ②.

BLOOMS: Male flowers come out in the autumn of the preceding year. In spring they form hanging yellow catkins ③. The inconspicuous female flowers occur at the very tips of the twig.

TYPICAL FEATURES

When rubbed between the fingers, the leaves of the Common Walnut may smell fragrant or unpleasant.

FRUIT: Green, oval fruit grow in pairs at the end of the branches. Botanically speaking they are stone fruit: the nut is the stone and the edible seed is the kernel ④.

DISTRIBUTION: Native to the eastern Mediterranean and South-east Asia; introduced to Central Europe as an agricultural plant by the Romans.

OTHER: Walnut trees can live for 500 years.

Horse Chestnut

Aesculus hippocastanum

DESCRIPTION: The deciduous Horse Chestnut, with its dense, spreading crown, can grow up to 30m tall ①. Its trunk divides just above ground level into numerous strong branches. The scales of its bark are coarse.

LEAVES: The leaves have a long central stalk and consist of five to seven leaflets meeting at a single base point ②. In autumn the foliage turns yellow.

TYPICAL FEATURES

Large, sticky, dark brown buds make the Horse Chestnut easy to identify in winter.

BLOOMS: The white flowers grow in tall candelabra up to 30cm long and have red and yellow spots.

FRUIT: The shiny brown seeds are contained in round, green shells with long spines ③.

DISTRIBUTION: Originally from South-eastern Europe and Western Asia; introduced to Europe as an ornamental tree and now widely established.

SIMILAR SPECIES: The Red-flowering Horse Chestnut (*Aesculus x carnea*) ④ is often planted in parkland; its fruit has few spines, if any.

Mistletoe

Viscum album

DESCRIPTION: The Mistletoe is an evergreen shrub, which grows on trees ① and can reach up to 1m in diameter. Its stems are green and forked.

LEAVES: Elongated, tough, leathery leaves form pairs on its stems ②.

BLOOMS: Male and female flowers grow on separate plants. They are minute and inconspicuous and are formed in the axil of the stems ③.

TYPICAL FEATURES
The Mistletoe is most visible high in the tree-tops in winter, when its host is bare of leaves.

FRUIT: Berries about the size of a pea ④ have a whitish, almost translucent flesh, which is very sticky and envelops one or more seeds.

DISTRIBUTION: Up to 1,300m altitude; only in areas with mild winters.

OTHER: The poisonous Mistletoe is a semi-parasite. It taps into the water system of the host and drains it of water and nutrient salts; its fruit is eaten by birds.

Weigela

Weigela florida

DESCRIPTION: The Weigela is a deciduous ornamental shrub growing to a height of 1–2m ①. Its long stems, inserted directly into the rootstock, are not very branched. Inside they are pithy. New stems grow from the root-stock every year.

LEAVES: Its long leaves ② are pointed and finely serrated. The ribs underneath the leaf are covered in hair, while the tops of the leaves are bare.

TYPICAL FEATURES
The shoots and young stems of the Weigela bear two distinctive rows of hairs.

BLOOMS: Abundant pinkish-red flowers are funnel-shaped and end in five distinct tips ④. They are either solitary or occur in dense panicles on short side shoots from the previous year's growth.

FRUIT: The carpels of the long brown capsules ③ open up when ripe to release the seeds.

DISTRIBUTION: East Asia; ornamental or garden shrub in Europe.

OTHER: Weigela occur in a very wide range of varieties. About 170 varieties have been cultivated from the ten known species.

Guelder Rose
Viburnum opulus

DESCRIPTION: The deciduous Guelder Rose is a bushy shrub ① growing 1–4m tall, with spreading, somewhat overhanging branches. It also occasionally grows as a small tree.

LEAVES: Its leaves have three to five lobes ② and are serrated at the margin; on their underside they carry a fine down. Their upper surface remains bare.

BLOOMS: In spring and occasionally again in autumn, the white flowers appear in broad, umbrella-like panicles ③. Whilst those at the extremities of the display form a large, star-shaped array, the inner flowers are smaller and bell-like.

FRUIT: Spherical, bright red stone fruits grow in dense clusters ④ and remain on the shrub until well into winter.

DISTRIBUTION: Thickets, woodland margins and lowland forests, often also planted as a garden specimen.

OTHER: The fruit of the Guelder Rose is mildly poisonous.

TYPICAL FEATURES
A display of nectar glands on the stalks of the leaves is a distinctive feature of the Guelder Rose.

Wayfaring Tree
Viburnum lantana

DESCRIPTION: The deciduous Wayfaring Tree is a bushy shrub growing 1–4m tall, whose stems grow erect and do not hang ①. The newest growth is densely covered with hair.

LEAVES: The short-stemmed leaves are ovoid and have sharply serrated margins ②. On their undersides they carry a dense grey mat of hairs.

BLOOMS: The white flowers rise in dense dome-shaped panicles ④. The individual flowers are similar in size; unlike the Guelder Rose it has no larger flowers at the extremities.

TYPICAL FEATURES
The Wayfaring Tree is best distinguished by handling its leaves, which have a soft, wrinkled feel.

FRUIT: The berry-like seeded fruits stand erect and as they ripen, they turn from green to red to black ③. They are shaped like an egg or extended oval, and are slightly compressed at the sides.

DISTRIBUTION: Woodland margins, open deciduous forests, thickets: often a garden specimen.

OTHER: The fruit of the Wayfaring Tree is mildly poisonous.

81

Mock Orange
Philadelphus coronarius

DESCRIPTION: The deciduous Mock Orange grows 1–3m in height; has erect branches and wand-like stems ①, which contain a soft pith.

LEAVES: The short-stemmed leaves are ovoid and pointed ③. Hairs grow on the veins on the underside of the leaf, whose margin is irregularly serrated.

BLOOMS: The white flowers measure 3–4cm across ② and grow in clusters at the end of the branches. Four petals are arranged around the numerous yellow stamen grouped in the centre of the flower.

FRUIT: The fruit is a brown capsule ④, which, when ripe, opens its four carpels to release numerous brown seeds.

DISTRIBUTION: The south-eastern Alps, from northern Italy to Western Asia; planted as an ornamental in Europe, and only rarely found growing in the wild.

OTHER: Certain garden varieties also bear flowers in clusters.

TYPICAL FEATURES

The Mock Orange develops a very intense perfume, especially in the evening.

Snowberry
Symphoricarpos rivularis

DESCRIPTION: The deciduous Snowberry is a bushy, many-branched shrub, which can grow up to 2m in height ①, with arching outer branches.

LEAVES: The simple leaves have smooth margins and are almost round ②. The underside of the leaf is somewhat paler than the top surface and is sometimes downy.

BLOOMS: The small bell-shaped flowers are white or dusky red ③ and grow profusely in dense clusters at the ends of branches or inserted in the axil between the leaf and stem.

FRUIT: White spherical stone fruits which can vary greatly in size ④. The juicy flesh of the fruit has a spongy consistency.

DISTRIBUTION: Native to western North America but introduced into Europe as an ornamental shrub. Very common in the wild.

OTHER: The fruit of the Snowberry is believed to be poisonous.

TYPICAL FEATURES

When crushed or squeezed, the fruit of the Snowberry bursts with an audible pop.

Forsythia
Forsythia x intermedia

DESCRIPTION: The Forsythia is a deciduous shrub that can reach 5m in height ① but is usually controlled by pruning in gardens and parks. The pale bark bears cork-like growths.

LEAVES: The long, narrow leaves ③ have smooth margins, or else are finely serrated.

BLOOMS: The showy yellow flowers ② appear in great abundance in spring, usually before the leaves. They are funnel shaped with four long, pointed petals.

FRUIT: Hard, brown capsules with two opening carpels form in summer.

TYPICAL FEATURES

Outside the flowering season, the pith in the stems is a distinctive feature of the Forsythia: it is split into individual cells ④.

DISTRIBUTION: East Asia; only occurs as an ornamental plant in central Europe.

OTHER: Forsythia is a cross between the Hanging Forsythia *(Forsythia suspensa)* and the Green Forsythia *(F. viridissima)* and was first discovered in the Göttingen Botanical Gardens in Germany, in the late 19th century.

Common Lilac
Syringa vulgaris

DESCRIPTION: The Common Lilac is a highly varied deciduous shrub reaching 2–6m in height ①, which also occurs as a tree with a rounded crown. Young wood has a smooth, green bark, while the bark of older branches is grey and furrowed.

LEAVES: The stalked leaves are oval and pointed, and cordate at the base ②. They are always hairless.

TYPICAL FEATURES

In winter, the Common Lilac can be distinguished by pairs of buds on the ends of its twigs ③.

BLOOMS: There are so many varieties of Lilac that white, blue and violet flowering examples are all common. The flowers grow in dense panicles ④ and have a pleasant fragrance. The conical displays usually have four spikes.

FRUIT: Brown bivalve capsules.

DISTRIBUTION: Originally a native of South-eastern Europe and the Near East; introduced into the United Kingdom in the Middle Ages and occasionally found in the wild; widespread today in over 900 garden varieties.

Common Buckthorn
Rhamnus cathartica

DESCRIPTION: The Common Buckthorn is a deciduous shrub growing up to 3m in height, or occasionally a small tree up to 8m tall ①. It branches irregularly and branches terminate in strong spines at their tips.

LEAVES: Simple oval leaves are pointed ③. The leaf margins are finely serrated and the veins follow an arc almost parallel to the margins.

BLOOMS: The shrub produces inconspicuous green, single-sex flowers ②. Both male and female occur on the same plant.

FRUIT: Matt black, pea-sized stone fruits grow in dense clusters ④.

DISTRIBUTION: Woodland margins, thickets, hedgerows and lowland forests.

OTHER: The fruit of the Common Buckthorn is poisonous and lethal cases have been known. Like the rest of the plant they contain laxative substances. Birds can consume them without coming to harm.

TYPICAL FEATURES
The stems of the Common Buckthorn are squarrose, i.e. opposite pairs of twigs form a 90 degree angle.

Common Privet | European Privet
Ligustrum vulgare

DESCRIPTION: The Common Privet is a shrub, which can grow to 3–4m in height ①. It can retain its green summer foliage until well into the winter and has thin and very flexible wand-like branches.

LEAVES: The short-stemmed leaves are oval-acute ②. They have a tough, leathery feel and a smooth margin. The underside is a paler green and has a pronounced central vein.

BLOOMS: Its small, white, four-petalled flowers ③ grow in sparse, upright panicles.

FRUIT: The spherical fruit starts out green and gradually turns a shiny blue-black ④.

DISTRIBUTION: At woodland margins, in thickets and lowland forests; widespread as a specimen plant.

OTHER: The fruit of the Common Privet, which remains on the shrub until winter, is unpleasant to humans, but very attractive to birds.

TYPICAL FEATURES
The Common Privet's floral display gives off an intense fragrance which not everyone finds pleasant.

Slender Deutzia
Deutzia gracilis

DESCRIPTION: The Slender Deutzia is a deciduous shrub up to 1m or so tall with a dense, bushy shape ①. Its ridged hollow stems grow in overhanging arches.

LEAVES: Elongated leaves taper at the base and have a few sharp serrations at their margins ②. The top surface is extremely hairy, while the underside is merely downy.

BLOOMS: The white flowers ④ have five petals arranged in a star shape and grow in slender panicles at the ends of the branches.

TYPICAL FEATURES

The stems of the Slender Deutzia are hollow. This feature distinguishes it from the similar Mock Orange (see p82), whose stems are pithy.

FRUIT: Relatively small, inconspicuous capsules are initially green ③, then turn brown and burst open when ripe.

DISTRIBUTION: Native to East Asia, especially Japan; introduced to Central Europe as an ornamental plant but not established in the wild.

OTHER: Deutzia are sold as garden ornamentals; certain varieties have pink or cluster flowers ①.

Butterfly Bush
Summer Lilac | *Buddleja davidii*

DESCRIPTION: The Butterfly Bush is a deciduous shrub with a spreading shape, which grows up to 3m in height ①. It has very long, gently hanging wand-like branches. Its new growth bears short hairs.

LEAVES: The long leaves can reach 25cm and are pointed ②. They are serrated at the margin and are silver-grey on the underside, where there is a felt-like mat of hairs.

TYPICAL FEATURES

Butterfly Bush flowers, which are rich in nectar, always attract butterflies in large numbers ④.

BLOOMS: In summer it displays purple to violet, or just occasionally white, flowers. They grow abundantly in dense panicles at the end of the branches, 10–30cm in length. The small individual flowers have four petals that fuse into a single tube.

FRUIT: Small, inconspicuous capsules ③.

DISTRIBUTION: Native to China and Japan; introduced as an ornamental shrub, later wild on waste ground and beside railways.

OTHER: A seedling can develop to a height of 2m within a year.

89

Black Honeysuckle
Lonicera nigra

DESCRIPTION: The black honeysuckle is a shrub that grows to one or two metres in height, and develops only a few branches ①. It has thin arching stems with a grey-brown bark. In winter its buds are small, black and surrounded by scales.

LEAVES: The short-stemmed leaves are long and oval ③ and never fused at their base. They are generally bare; hair can only be observed on the veins, if at all.

TYPICAL FEATURES
The Black Honeysuckle's round berries grow together at the base.

BLOOMS: The white flowers, often with a reddish blush, grow in pairs in the axils of the leaves ④. Each flower has four upper lips and one lower.

FRUIT: Pairs of round berries ripen to a bluish-black on a stalk 2–3cm long ②. They sometimes differ in size.

DISTRIBUTION: Woodland margins, footpaths, thickets; very common in upland areas.

OTHER: Black Honeysuckle berries are poisonous.

Fly Honeysuckle
Lonicera xylosteum

DESCRIPTION: The Fly Honeysuckle is a deciduous shrub growing 1–3m in height ①. Its branches grow profusely and if left unchecked, it spreads into a bush.

LEAVES: Stalked leaves are oval or ovoid ② and bear a fine down on their top surfaces and undersides. The margins also carry small hairs. Opposite leaves never fuse at their base.

TYPICAL FEATURES
The Fly Honeysuckle is distinguished by its downy leaves and shiny dark red berries.

BLOOMS: The fragrant, yellowish-white flowers ③ grow in pairs on a stalk in the leaf axils. The stamen are clearly visible in the space between the four-lipped upper frill and the undivided lower lip.

FRUIT: Pea-sized dark red berries ④ grow in pairs on a single stalk, but are unfused.

DISTRIBUTION: In the undergrowth of mixed deciduous and coniferous forests.

OTHER: Fruit of the Fly Honeysuckle is mildly poisonous.

Common Honeysuckle
Lonicera periclymenum

DESCRIPTION: The deciduous Common Honeysuckle is a climbing shrub with dense foliage that grows creeper-like to a height of four to five metres ① on vertical surfaces.

LEAVES: The leaves grow on a short stem ② and also directly on the branches, but remain unfused. They are elongated to oval and on their lower surface they have a faint blue shimmer.

BLOOMS: The white or yellowish tubular flowers ③ grow to 5cm in length and are formed from an upper and lower lip. Their stamen project far out of the flower.

TYPICAL FEATURES
Unlike the Fly Honeysuckle (see p90) the flowers and berries of the Common Honeysuckle do not grow in single pairs but in clusters.

FRUIT: The bright red berries ④ grow in pairs, with several pairs of berries forming a cluster.

DISTRIBUTION: In hedgerows and thickets, at woodland margins.

OTHER: The fruit of the Common Honeysuckle is mildly poisonous.

Perfoliate Honeysuckle
Garden Honeysuckle
Lonicera caprifolium

DESCRIPTION: The deciduous Perfoliate Honeysuckle is a creeper that can reach up to 5m ①. The creeping stems twine dextrally around their climbing base.

LEAVES: The lower leaves are either on a short stalk ② or grow directly on the twigs. The upper pair of leaves fuse together at their base, which gives the impression that the stalk is protruding through a plate-like leaf.

TYPICAL FEATURES
Perched on their plate-like leaves, the flowers of the Honeysuckle are very fragrant from early evening onwards.

BLOOMS: The white or yellowish flowers ③, which have a reddish blush, usually grow in clusters of six on the upper two or three pairs of leaves. They are characterised by their four upper and single, undivided lower lips.

FRUIT: Spherical, coral pink berries ④ are unfused and form small clusters.

DISTRIBUTION: In open woodland and thickets; originally from South-eastern Europe but introduced early to Central Europe and now common in the wild.

OTHER: The red berries of the Perfoliate Honeysuckle are poisonous.

93

Broad-leaved Spindle Tree
Euonymus latifolia

DESCRIPTION: The Broad-leaved Spindle Tree, with its erect branches ①, is a shrub or occasionally a small tree, which grows up to 5m tall.
LEAVES: The oval leaves ③ are pointed and their margins finely serrated.
BLOOMS: Flowers grow in small racemes with long stems ②. They are no more than 5–7mm across and are greenish or sometimes brownish in colour with four or five petals.
FRUIT: The four or five valved capsules are red to violet in colour; beneath each valve is a white seed with a red-orange coating. When fully ripe, the seeds hang free of their capsules ④.
DISTRIBUTION: Native to forests and mountains in southern Europe.
OTHER: The conspicuous fruit is highly poisonous.

TYPICAL FEATURES
The branches of the Broad-leaved Spindle Tree are round in section. A groove-like depression is a feature of the leaf stems.

Spindle Tree
Euonymus europaea

DESCRIPTION: The deciduous Spindle Tree develops into either a densely branched shrub or a small tree ①, but in neither case does it exceed 6m in height.
LEAVES: Oval leaves ② are finely serrated and pointed. In autumn the foliage turns a vivid copper red ①.
BLOOMS: The long-stemmed flowers ③ form in the axils of the leaves. Their four white petals grow in the shape of a cross.
FRUIT: Conspicuous red capsules have four valves, each of which drops a single seed shrouded in a bright orange-red coating ④.
DISTRIBUTION: On open, nutrient-rich ground; woodland and wayside margins, hedgerows; widespread throughout Europe.
OTHER: The fruit of the Spindle Tree is highly poisonous to humans. Birds, by contrast, are very keen on the fruit and can consume it without coming to harm.

TYPICAL FEATURES
The Spindle Tree is distinguished from the Broad-leaved Spindle Tree by its quadrangular stems and a strip-like growth of cork along new stems.

Box Tree

Buxus sempervirens

DESCRIPTION: The evergreen Box Tree develops into a very densely branching shrub about 5m tall ①. It also grows in tree form, but rarely reaches more than 10m in height.

LEAVES: Oval leaves ④ are only 1–2cm long. They grow very close to the branches on short stalks. As a rule, the top surface of the leaf is a darker green than the underside.

BLOOMS: Small yellowish flowers are densely packed in the axils of the leaves. Male and female flowers ② grow side by side.

FRUIT: The small, hard capsules ③ are brown when ripe.

DISTRIBUTION: On dry, sunny slopes, on crags and in open woodland; usually in dry soil; often used for hedging. The wood is popular in Christmas wreaths.

OTHER: All parts of the Box Tree are mildly poisonous.

TYPICAL FEATURES

The combination of densely packed oval leaves and axillary flowers is typical of this particular species of Box Tree.

Indian Bean Tree

Catalpa bignonioides

DESCRIPTION: The deciduous Indian Bean Tree grows up to 15m tall ①. Its spreading crown springs from a short trunk. Its bark is grey-brown and divided into flaky strips.

LEAVES: Leaves measure up to 25cm in length and are formed on a long stalk ②. They are rounded and cordate at the base and have a pronounced point. When rubbed they have an unpleasant smell.

BLOOMS: White or yellowish flowers ④, 3–5cm across, grow profusely in erect panicles. They are bell-shaped with a frilled edge and are flecked with yellow and red inside.

TYPICAL FEATURES

Remaining on the tree until well into winter, the unusually long fruit, which is about the thickness of a pencil, is a reliable distinguishing feature of the Indian Bean Tree.

FRUIT: Its straight, light brown capsules ③, which grow to 40cm long, are reminiscent of beans or thin cigars.

DISTRIBUTION: South-eastern North America; introduced here as an ornamental tree for parks and gardens.

97

Cornelian Cherry

Cornus mas

DESCRIPTION: The deciduous Cornelian cherry grows as either a loosely branching shrub ① or a small tree up to 8m in height.

LEAVES: The simple oval leaves are pointed with a smooth margin and pronounced curving veins on their surface ③. Both the upper and lower leaf surfaces are covered in fine hair.

BLOOMS: The yellow flowers appear long before the leaves. They grow in small umbels directly on the twigs ②. Beneath the display of flowers, there are four bracts arranged in the shape of a cross.

TYPICAL FEATURES

Its early flowering season and the typical leaves with their curving veins make the Cornelian Cherry easy to distinguish.

FRUIT: In summer, bright red stone fruits about the size of a grape ④ hang from the twigs.

DISTRIBUTION: At woodland margins, in open woodland, hedgerows and thickets; also planted in parks and streets.

OTHER: The red fruit of the Cornelian Cherry is edible.

Dogwood

Cornus sanguinea

DESCRIPTION: The deciduous Dogwood is a shrub that grows up to 5m in height ① or a small tree. In winter in particular, the bark of the branches turns red where it faces the sun.

LEAVES: The simple oval leaves with short stems are pointed ②. Their veins curve parallel to the margin. In autumn the foliage turns a vivid red.

TYPICAL FEATURES

The delicate white flowers of the Dogwood secrete a substance with a fishy smell.

BLOOMS: The white flowers appear once the leaves are out. They grow in dense spreading panicles ③ and each individual flower has four bracts.

FRUIT: Pea-sized stone fruits ④ ripen from autumn onwards. Initially they are green or red, later turning to black. The stalks of the fruit are a vivid red.

DISTRIBUTION: In hedgerows and sparse lowland forests, at woodland margins; in nutrient-rich, dryish soil.

OTHER: Unlike the Cornelian Cherry, the fruit of the Dogwood is unsuitable for human consumption, though birds find them very attractive.

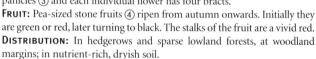

99

Field Maple | Common Maple
Acer campestre

DESCRIPTION: The deciduous Field Maple is a tree with a domed crown, which grows up to 20m in height ①; however, it is often smaller, in which case it is more like a shrub. The bark of the trunk is grey-brown and divided into rectangular patches ③.

LEAVES: Simple leaves are divided into five, or less commonly three, lobes ②. Their foremost lobes are generally also cleft.

BLOOMS: Small, yellow-green flowers grow in hanging panicles at the ends of twigs. Each individual flower has five oval petals.

TYPICAL FEATURES
Wand-like shoots often spring from the older growth of the Field Maple. The stalks of leaves and young shoots contain a milky sap.

FRUIT: Fruit grows in a double samara ④, with wings at 180 degrees forming a straight line.

DISTRIBUTION: The margins of mixed deciduous woodland, in thickets and hedgerows; usually in nutrient-rich soil.

French Maple
Acer monspessulanum

DESCRIPTION: The French Maple is a deciduous tree, which grows to about 10m tall ①, but which also occurs as a shrub. Its branches are generally twisted and erect.

LEAVES: Long-stemmed, somewhat leathery leaves are divided into three lobes of about equal size ②. Bushy hairs can be discerned in the angle between the veins on the underside of the leaves. In autumn the foliage turns a vivid yellow, or less commonly red.

TYPICAL FEATURES
The almost parallel wings of the paired fruits are a distinguishing feature of the French Maple.

BLOOMS: Small, yellow-green, bell-shaped flowers ③ appear in spring at the same time as the leaves. They grow in panicles at the ends of twigs and each has four petals.

FRUIT: The winged fruits, known as samaras, hang in pairs ④. Their wings lie parallel to each other or form a very acute angle. When ripe, the wings are brown-red in colour.

DISTRIBUTION: Southern Europe; in Central Europe only in very mild regions e.g. wine growing areas, on warm, dry slopes.

Sycamore
Acer pseudoplatanus

DESCRIPTION: The deciduous Sycamore is a tree, which grows up to 35m tall ①. Its broad, rounded crown rises above a powerful, straight trunk. The trunks of older trees shed flat flakes of bark ③.

LEAVES: Long, simple leaves ② grow up to 20cm long and across. They are five-lobed, the three central lobes being significantly larger than the two outer lobes. In autumn the foliage turns a golden yellow.

BLOOMS: The small, yellow-green flowers grow in long, hanging panicles at the ends of young twigs.

FRUIT: The winged samaras hang in pairs ④, the wings forming a near right-angle.

DISTRIBUTION: Throughout the Near East, southern Europe and the Caucasus; elsewhere planted in parks and avenues.

TYPICAL FEATURES

Short, pointed teeth at the leaf margins are a feature of the Sycamore. The five lobes of the leaf meet each other at a very acute angle.

Japanese Maple
Acer palmatum

DESCRIPTION: The deciduous Japanese Maple is a small tree or shrub 6–8m in height ①. Its curving branches thrust upwards to form a broad, spreading crown. When bare of leaves, it bears conspicuous, bulbous red buds ②.

LEAVES: Simple leaves are divided into five or seven lobes ④. Each lobe is pointed and toothed at the margin.

BLOOMS: Minute, red flowers with five petals grow in erect or nodding panicles.

FRUIT: Winged light brown samaras hang in pairs ③. The wings meet at a divergent angle.

DISTRIBUTION: China, Japan, Korea; introduced here as an ornamental species.

OTHER: A great many cultivated varieties are commercially available, varying widely in their form and the colour of their foliage.

TYPICAL FEATURES

In autumn, the characteristic, deeply divided leaves of the Japanese Maple turn a bright yellow or scarlet.

Norway Maple
Acer platanoides

DESCRIPTION: The deciduous Norway Maple is a tree that grows up to 30m in height ①. Its rounded crown is formed of strong erect branches. The bark is dark grey and ridged.

LEAVES: Simple leaves are divided into five lobes, with rounded clefts ②. The three central lobes are about equal in size and serrated. The stalks of the leaves contain a milky sap.

BLOOMS: The yellow-green flowers ③ appear before the leaves. They are joined at the ends of twigs in umbellate panicles.

FRUIT: Winged samaras hang in pairs ④. The wings meet at a divergent angle.

DISTRIBUTION: In mixed and lowland forest, from the plain up to an altitude of about 1,100m; also planted as an ornamental shrub and in parks and avenues.

TYPICAL FEATURES
The Norway Maple has similar fruit and sap-bearing stalks to the Field or Common Maple (see p100), but its leaves are five-lobed and drawn out into points.

Silver Maple
Acer saccharinum

DESCRIPTION: The deciduous Silver Maple can reach a height of 25–30m ①, but is often smaller. Its irregular crown is formed of a mass of erect branches. Young twigs are somewhat pendulous. It often grows with a divided trunk.

LEAVES: Simple leaves are deeply divided into five pointed lobes. Each lobe is itself irregularly serrated ④. In autumn the foliage turns a vivid yellow. By contrast with the Norway Maple, the stalks of its leaves contain no sap.

TYPICAL FEATURES
The underside of the leaves of the Silver Maple are pale and covered in silvery hairs ②.

BLOOMS: The flowers appear in spring, before the leaves. Male and female flowers occur on the same specimen, but in separate umbels.

FRUIT: The double samaras have twisted, sabre-like wings, which join at a near right-angle.

DISTRIBUTION: Native to lowland forests of eastern North America; introduced to parks in Europe.

Cowberry

Vaccinium vitis-idaea

DESCRIPTION: An evergreen dwarf shrub reaching a maximum height of 30cm. It is a creeping plant with curved branches. Young branches are green and round.

LEAVES: Short-stemmed leaves are perfectly oval with a smooth edge, often curved slightly under. Upper surface of the leaf is shiny dark-green, but underside ④ is lighter and matt.

BLOOMS: The white flower petals are pink on the outside and curve outwards. The flowers form hanging racemes at the ends of the branches ②. Each individual bell-shaped bloom ③ ends in four points.

TYPICAL FEATURES
The Cowberry is easy to identify by its racemes of bell-shaped flowers and by its bright red berries.

FRUITS: The berries are about 1cm long and are initially a greenish-white, changing to a bright red when ripe ①.

DISTRIBUTION: On the edges of moors, in light conifer woodland and in heathland covered with dwarf shrubs in high mountain ranges.

OTHER: Cowberries are edible and are rich in Vitamin C.

Common Bearberry

Arctostaphylos uva-ursi

DESCRIPTION: The evergreen Common Bearberry is a low-lying shrub. It has densely forked branches, which grow to cover the ground like a carpet. The branches are very stiff, with a brown-red bark.

LEAVES: The short-stemmed, oval leaves have smooth edges and are very stiff and leathery. They are shiny green on top, and the underside ② is paler green with a lattice of leaf veins.

TYPICAL FEATURES
Unlike the similar Cowberry, the Common Bearberry leaves have a prominent lattice of veins on the underside.

BLOOMS: The white flowers grow in small racemes at the tips of the branches ④. The individual flowers consist of five petals which grow together as one, leaving a small opening ③.

FRUITS: The spherical, bright red berries ripen in summer ①.

DISTRIBUTION: Rare in the mountain ranges of the United Kingdom but more common in the Alps; also found on the tundra of Northern Europe and Asia.

OTHER: The berries of the Common Bearberry are inedible. The species is endangered and protected.

Bilberry | Blueberry
Vaccinium myrtillus

DESCRIPTION: The Bilberry is a deciduous dwarf shrub with heavily forked branches that can reach a height of 50cm. The roots send out side shoots, which develop into new plants, and over time grow to cover large areas.

LEAVES: The short-stemmed, oval leaves have delicate, serrated edges ③. They change from green to red in autumn. Prominent leaf veins can be seen on the lighter underside.

BLOOMS: The red flowers have curved lips ④ and are located individually where the leaf joins the branch. The petals grow to form a sphere, only leaving a small opening.

FRUITS: The dark blue berries ① are plump and contain blue flesh and juice.

DISTRIBUTION: Light conifer woodland, moorland and heathland.

OTHER: Bilberries have a pleasant taste and are rich in Vitamin C.

TYPICAL FEATURES
The branches of the Bilberry are only wooden at the base. Younger branches are green and flexible and have wing-like edges ②.

Bog Bilberry | Bog Blueberry
Vaccinium uliginosum

DESCRIPTION: The Bog Bilberry is a deciduous dwarf shrub that can reach a height of 75cm. It has creeping branches, which divide heavily into smaller branches. The shrub can cover large areas. Only the newest shoots have a green bark.

LEAVES: The stemmed, oval leaves ③ have a smooth edge, which can sometimes be slightly thicker than the rest of the leaf. Leaf veins are prominent on the underside.

BLOOMS: The cup-shaped flowers have pink and white petals with curled edges ④. They are arranged in small numbers where the uppermost leaves join the branch.

FRUITS: The blue, plump berries ① can be as much as 1cm thick and have a light flesh and juice.

DISTRIBUTION: In moors, bogs and conifer woodland, and in the Alps.

OTHER: The fruits are edible, but have little flavour. If eaten in large quantities, they are said to have a slightly narcotic effect.

TYPICAL FEATURES
Unlike the very similar Bilberry, the Bog Bilberry has rounded branches with a grey to red-brown bark ②.

Dwarf Birch

Betula nana

DESCRIPTION: The Dwarf Birch is a low-growing, deciduous dwarf shrub, which can reach a height of 50cm ①. Older branches have a rough, dark brown bark; younger branches have dense, soft hairs.

LEAVES: The short-stemmed, almost circular leaves are the size and shape of small coins ②. The edges have rounded serrations.

BLOOMS: Male and female catkins are located upright on the branches; female catkins ③ are a slightly darker yellow than the male.

FRUITS: The small nuts have thin wings and are arranged in light-green, vertical fruit clusters on the branches ④.

DISTRIBUTION: In peaty, wet soil in moorland; in Northern and Central Europe and in the Alps.

OTHER: As marshland in Central Europe is being drained, the Dwarf Birch is becoming a rare and protected species.

TYPICAL FEATURES
The leaves of the Dwarf Birch are slightly sticky. In autumn they turn bright orange.

Creeping Willow

Salix repens

DESCRIPTION: The Creeping Willow is a deciduous shrub that can grow to a height of 1m ①. Several branches grow out from the creeping trunk and further divide into dense twigs. It can grow to cover large areas.

LEAVES: The short-stemmed, long leaves have a smooth edge, which curves slightly under ②. The underside has soft hairs, and young leaves also have hairs on the upper surface.

BLOOMS: The flowers appear shortly before the leaves. Male and female catkins are positioned upright on different plants. Yellow stamen extend from the male catkins ③. Female catkins are a greenish colour.

FRUITS: The small, light brown capsule fruits burst in summer and release large numbers of seeds with long white hairs ④.

DISTRIBUTION: On lowland moors, damp, coarse pasture and heathland; also in marshy areas around coastal dunes.

TYPICAL FEATURES
The leaves of the Creeping Willow are only 1–4cm long and no more than 2cm wide. They have soft grey hairs on the underside.

Needle Furze | Needle Genista
Genista anglica

DESCRIPTION: The Needle Furze is a deciduous shrub with a small number of branches, which grows to a height of 50cm. Older branches have long spines ③, and are often free of leaves. Younger branches have ridges.

LEAVES: The narrow, short-stemmed leaves have smooth edges and no hairs ②.

BLOOMS: The yellow flowers ① are characteristic of the pea family: the two lower petals grow together to form a boat-like structure, two further petals are located like wings on either side, and a fifth petal stands upright.

TYPICAL FEATURES

The Needle Furze can be easily identified by its spiny branches and hairless leaves. Only the flowering shoots have no spines.

FRUITS: The light brown, hairless pods are roughly 2cm long.

DISTRIBUTION: Atlantic coast of Western and Central Europe; in lowland heaths, moors and in light pine woodland.

SIMILAR SPECIES: Hairy Greenweed (*Genista pilosa*) ④ has similar flowers, but its leaves have dense hairs on the underside.

German Broom
Genista germanica

DESCRIPTION: The German Broom is a compact, deciduous shrub, which can reach a height of 60 cm ④. The older, creeping branches have spines and only rarely have leaves ③; the younger branch shoots grow vertically and have perpendicular hairs ①.

LEAVES: The long, oval leaves have short stems or attach directly to the branch ②. The edges of the underside of the leaves have long hairs.

TYPICAL FEATURES

Unlike the Needle Furze, the leaves and young branches of the German Broom are covered in hairs.

BLOOMS: The yellow flowers form in long racemes at the tips of the branches ①. Two petals grow together to form a ship-like structure, two small wing petals form either side, and a fifth petal stands upright in the middle.

FRUITS: The pods are slightly more than 1cm long and turn dark-brown when mature. They are densely covered in long hairs.

DISTRIBUTION: In meadows and on heaths, in open woodland and on footpath verges; in dry, stony soil.

OTHER: The seeds contain essential oils, as well as poisons.

Dyers' Greenweed
Dyers' Broom
Genista tinctoria

DESCRIPTION: Dyers' Greenweed is a deciduous shrub, which can grow to a height of 1m ① and which has vertical, rod-shaped, fluted branches that are only woody at the base.

LEAVES: The narrow, pointed leaves are attached directly to the young branches ②. They have smooth edges and soft hairs.

BLOOMS: The yellow flowers are arranged in large numbers on upright racemes ④. The individual flowers consist of a narrow, boat-like structure, two wing petals on either side and a fifth petal standing vertically above the rest.

TYPICAL FEATURES
Dyers' Greenweed has distinctly fluted, green branches with no spines. Normally only the upper part of the plant bears leaves.

FRUITS: The pods can be as long as 3cm, but are only 3mm wide and very flat ③. They burst open when mature, releasing the seeds.

DISTRIBUTION: On heathland and rough pasture; also in light woodland.

OTHER: Contains toxic alkaloids. The yellow colouring is still used as a dye.

Japanese Kerria
Japanese Rose | Kerria Rose
Kerria japonica

DESCRIPTION: The deciduous Japanese Kerria can reach a height of 50–200cm ①. Its straight branches have a shiny, green bark, grow vertically and sprout next to each other, directly from the rootstock. Each branch has short side-branches. The core of the branches contains a thick, white pith.

TYPICAL FEATURES
The Japanese Kerria can be identified by its green bark, serrated leaves and yellow flowers, which are rounded in its ornamental form.

LEAVES: The short-stemmed, oval leaves end in a long point ②. They have a deep, double serration. The upper surface of the leaf is always hairless, but the underside can sometimes have sparse hairs.

BLOOMS: The five yellow petals are spread flat ③. In their centre stand numerous stamen. Ornamental varieties have fuller flowers with numerous petals ④; the flower then appears more spherical.

FRUITS: The small, individual stone fruits are unremarkable.

DISTRIBUTION: Native to China, in the undergrowth of light woodland; in Europe it is planted almost exclusively as an ornamental.

115

Sweet Gale | Bog Myrtle
Myrica gale

DESCRIPTION: Sweet Gale is a bushy, deciduous shrub, about 50–100cm in height ①. Its branches are rod-shaped and grow vertically, but have numerous side-branches.

LEAVES: The leathery, short-stemmed leaves are long and taper noticeably towards the stem ②. The top and underside of the leaves have slight hairs, and the leaf edge is serrated near the tip.

TYPICAL FEATURES
Sweet Gale releases an intense aroma if you rub the branches.

BLOOMS: The flowers are formed before the leaves. The yellow-brown male flowers ④ and the green-yellow female flowers ③ are found in catkins on different plants. Male catkins are oblong and about 1cm long; female catkins are oval.

FRUITS: The tiny stone fruits form in brown fruit clusters.

DISTRIBUTION: On wet heathland moors, in damp heathland and on the edges of moorland; mainly in lowland areas.

OTHER: Leaves and flowers contain a poisonous essential oil.

Mezereon
Daphne mezereum

DESCRIPTION: Mezereon is a deciduous shrub, with sparse branches, which can reach a height of 1m. Its rod-shaped branches grow upwards.

LEAVES: The short-stemmed, soft leaves are arranged in dense whorls at the branch tips. They are long and and taper towards the stem to form a wedge-shape ②. Young leaves have short hairs on their edges.

TYPICAL FEATURES
The Mezereon's flowers have such a strong aroma that they can be smelt from several metres away.

BLOOMS: The pink to dark-red flowers have four petals ③ and form long before the first leaves. They are attached directly to the branch in dense clusters ④.

FRUITS: The juice-filled, spherical stone fruits are initially green, but turn red when ripe ①. They contain a single seed.

DISTRIBUTION: In deciduous and mixed woodland, from lowland areas to the Alps.

OTHER: Mezereon is a protected plant. All parts of the plant contain strong poisons. Simple contact with liquid from the leaves or fruit is enough to cause a skin irritation that can take a long time to heal.

Gooseberry
Ribes uva-crispa

DESCRIPTION: The Gooseberry is a bushy deciduous shrub, which can grow to a height of 50–150cm ①. Young branches have hairs.

LEAVES: Stemmed, hairy leaves have between three and five lobes and serrated edges ②. Both leaf surfaces are covered in short hairs.

BLOOMS: Green to red coloured flowers ③ form individually or in small racemes. Each flower has five hairy sepals and five petals.

FRUITS: The translucent, green berries ④ can be up to 2cm long and contain juice. The fruits of cultivated varieties can have a slight red colouring.

TYPICAL FEATURES
Gooseberry branches have individual thorns, or even double and treble thorns, which can be up to 1cm long and are very sharp.

DISTRIBUTION: In lowland forest and light thickets; often planted in gardens as a berry bush.

OTHER: There are numerous garden varieties, each with their distinct growing shape and size, and these often fruit at a different time to the wild plants.

Mountain Currant
Ribes alpinum

DESCRIPTION: The Mountain Currant is a deciduous shrub with dense branches, which can grow to a height of 1–2m ①. Its branches have a pale bark and no spines.

LEAVES: The stemmed leaves have between three and five lobes ②. Each lobe ends in a point and has serrated edges but no hairs.

BLOOMS: The green-yellow flowers form on upright racemes ③. Male and female flowers are often found on the same plant, and in such cases, the female racemes are smaller. The individual flowers have four or five small petals.

TYPICAL FEATURES
The leaf stems of the Mountain Currant are half as long as the leaves and have hairs.

FRUITS: The juicy berry fruits turn red when ripe ④.

DISTRIBUTION: Mainly in the Alps, but also in other mountain ranges, gorge woodland and on cliffs; almost never found in lowland areas.

OTHER: The berries of the Mountain Currant are edible, but have little flavour. The shrub can survive pollution and regular pruning and is therefore often used as a hedgerow plant.

119

Black Currant
Ribes nigrum

DESCRIPTION: The Black Currant is a decidu-ous, upright-growing shrub, which can reach a height of 1–2m. Young branches have hairs.

LEAVES: The long-stemmed leaves have between three and five lobes and are heart-shaped where the stem attaches to the leaf ②. The leaf edges are serrated, and the leaf veins have short hairs. The underside has yellow, gland-like markings.

> **TYPICAL FEATURES**
> If you crush Black Cur-rant leaves between your fingers, a strong aromatic fragrance is released.

BLOOMS: The green-yellow flowers form in upright or hanging racemes ④. The sepals form a bell-shape and turn slightly outwards at the rim; they are longer than the five petals ③.

FRUITS: The spherical berry fruits ① become a matt black colour when ripe.

DISTRIBUTION: Lowland forest, damp thickets on river banks; often planted as a berry bush and crops then become wild.

OTHER: The Black Currant or Blackcurrant is rich in Vitamin C.

Red Currant
Ribes rubrum

DESCRIPTION: The Red Currant is a decidu-ous, upright-growing shrub, which can reach a height of 1–2m. Wild varieties also form creep-ing shoots. Young branches have light hairs.

LEAVES: The long-stemmed leaves have between three and five lobes, with serrated edges ②.

> **TYPICAL FEATURES**
> Red Currant leaves can be distinguished from Black Currant leaves because they do not have yellow gland-like spots. They also have no aroma.

BLOOMS: The green-yellow flowers form in small racemes ③. The sepals form a bell-shape and are longer than the petals.

FRUITS: The pea-sized berries turn red when ripe ① and hang in bunches from the branch.

DISTRIBUTION: Lowland forests and river banks; often planted as a bush.

OTHER: Redcurrants do not contain much sugar and have much less Vitamin C than the Blackcurrant.

SIMILAR SPECIES: The Flowering Currant (*Ribes sanguineum*) originates from North America. Its red flowers ④ make it a popular ornamental shrub.

Green Alder
Alnus viridis

DESCRIPTION: A deciduous shrub, growing to a height of 50–250cm. Branches spread broadly. Forms offshoots and can cover large areas. Very occasionally grows in tree form.

LEAVES: The stemmed, oval leaves end in a point ②. Their edges have a double serration, meaning that each tooth-like indentation is itself further indented. The underside of the leaves carry tufts of hairs in between the veins.

TYPICAL FEATURES
The cone-like fruit clusters are typical for all Alders. The Green Alder differs from other Alder varieties because of its pointed leaves.

BLOOMS: The male flowers form yellow catkins up to 6cm long, which hang limply from the branch ①; the female catkins are red ③ and stand upright on the tips of the branches.

FRUITS: The cone-like fruit clusters ④ are initially green and become brown with age. They remain on the shrub for a long time.

DISTRIBUTION: In low mountain ranges and up to an altitude of 2400m; only grows on damp to humid soil.

Eared Sallow | Eared Willow
Salix aurita

DESCRIPTION: The Eared Sallow is a compact deciduous bush, with loose branches, which can reach a height of 2m ①. Branches grow upright; young branches have hairs and an almost black bark.

LEAVES: The round leaves are widest in the final third furthest from the stem ②. They end in a short, twisting tip. The undersides have curly hairs; the top of the leaves only have slight hairs.

TYPICAL FEATURES
The Eared Sallow forms kidney-shaped stipules where the leaf-stems join the branch.

BLOOMS: The flowers appear in spring before the leaves. Male and female catkins ④ are found on different plants. The female catkins are 3cm long, making them slightly larger than the male catkins.

FRUITS: Fruits ripen in summer in the catkins. All of the tiny seeds are entirely covered in white hairs ③.

DISTRIBUTION: Banks and ditches, damp meadows and fens.

OTHER: The Eared Sallow can form crossbreeds with other varieties of willow. The resulting plants have varying growth forms.

123

Wild Common Cotoneaster
Cotoneaster integerrimus

DESCRIPTION: The Wild Common Cotoneaster is an evergreen shrub, which can reach a height of 1m. It has upright, dense branches. Young branches have felt-like hairs.

LEAVES: The stemmed, oval leaves ② are arranged in two rows. They have smooth edges and are white on the underside, or they sometimes have grey hairs. When the leaves are unfurled, they appear to be brilliant white on the tips of the branches ④.

BLOOMS: Small, white flowers have a slight red colouring ③ and appear individually where the leaf joins the branch, or in small numbers at the branch tips. The individual flowers have five sepals and petals and the sepals have hairy edges.

FRUITS: The pea-sized red berries ① are inedible.

DISTRIBUTION: Eastern Mediterranean and southern Europe, on cliffs, rocky outcrops and scree. Grown as an ornamental in the UK.

TYPICAL FEATURES
Wild Common Cotoneaster can be identified by its felty hairs on the underside of the leaves and its smooth, red-brown bark on older branches.

Japanese Quince
Chaenomeles japonica

DESCRIPTION: The deciduous Japanese Quince is a shrub, growing to a height of 1m ①. Its branches are densely forked and sometimes have spines, but are generally spineless.

LEAVES: Oval, short-stemmed leaves ② have a leathery texture. Edges are smooth or have slight serration. The underside of the leaves is always a lighter green than the upper surface.

BLOOMS: Large, striking, flat flowers ④ form in racemes and on the branch tips. Each of the red flowers consists of five petals, with several yellow stamen extending from the centre.

TYPICAL FEATURES
The round fruits of the Japanese Quince have a felt-like coating, and can be identified by their aromatic fragrance.

FRUITS: The spherical apple fruits ③ have a diameter of 4cm and have a green-yellow skin.

DISTRIBUTION: Native to East Asia; in Central Europe planted as an ornamental plant.

OTHER: The fruits of the Japanese Quince are edible, but very sour. They are often cooked and made into jams.

125

Common Barberry

Berberis vulgaris

DESCRIPTION: The deciduous Common Barberry can reach a height of 1–3m ①. It grows with long, curved, overhanging branches, which bear 2cm-long, triple spines ③.

LEAVES: The stemmed, small leaves are arranged in groups. They are elliptical and taper towards the stem. They are rounded towards the tip and and have serrated edges.

TYPICAL FEATURES

The Common Barberry has characteristic angular, grooved branches, which bear triple spines.

BLOOMS: The small, yellow, strong smelling flowers form in short racemes ②. The round petals grow together to form a spherical shape.

FRUITS: The oblong, bright red berries ④ form in hanging clusters and are about 1cm long.

DISTRIBUTION: Coppices, hedgerows, forest edges, lanes and clearings.

OTHER: In rural areas, the Common Barberry has been almost completely eradicated, because it carries rust fungus, which can cause crops to fail.

Firethorn

Pyracantha coccinea

DESCRIPTION: The Firethorn is a shrub that keeps its green leaves in winter and which can reach a height of 1–3m. It grows with vertical branches, located far apart, which have long spines ③.

LEAVES: The stemmed leaves ② have a leathery texture. The are long and oval and end in a blunt or spiny tip. The upper surface of the leaf is shiny green, and the underside is matt. The edges have a rounded serration.

TYPICAL FEATURES

When not in fruit, the Firethorn can be identified by its long spines. The flower clusters have a strong smell.

BLOOMS: The cream-white flowers form in very large numbers in umbel-like, flat racemes ④. The Firethorn quite frequently has a second bloom in autumn.

FRUITS: The round, berry-like apple fruits are about 5mm think and have an orange to scarlet red colouring ①.

DISTRIBUTION: Native in south-east Europe, from the Balkans to the Black Sea; planted throughout the United Kingdom as an ornamental.

OTHER: The Firethorn is thought to be poisonous though birds love it.

Cherry Laurel
Prunus laurocerasus

DESCRIPTION: The evergreen Cherry Laurel is a shrub, which can reach a height of 1–5m and which has upright branches. In the wild it can also develop into a small tree.

LEAVES: The long, oval leaves are up to 15cm long and leathery ③. They form on short stems and are shiny green on the upper surface, and matt on the underside. The smooth leaf edges roll under slightly.

TYPICAL FEATURES

The Cherry Laurel's leathery leaves with rolled edges smell a bit like bitter almond when crushed.

BLOOMS: White flowers appear in large numbers in upright racemes up to 15cm tall ①. Five round petals fold back widely when flower is open, and the stamen radiate out from the centre ④.

FRUITS: The pea-sized stone fruits ② are black when ripe.

DISTRIBUTION: In South-east Europe and Asia Minor; grows in light deciduous woodland and shady glades; introduced into the United Kingdom as an ornamental shrub.

OTHER: All parts of the Cherry Laurel are poisonous.

Blackthorn | Sloe
Prunus spinosa

DESCRIPTION: The Blackthorn is a deciduous shrub, which reaches a height of 1–3m ①. Branches grow upright or slightly outwards and divide into numerous smaller branches. Long spines appear on shorter branches ③.

LEAVES: The small, stemmed leaves ② are often arranged together in groups. They are oval and have slightly serrated edges.

BLOOMS: The white flowers appear long before the leaves and are located close to the smaller branches. Each flower has five petals surrounding numerous stamen.

TYPICAL FEATURES

When the tree is not in bloom or in fruit, the Blackthorn can be identified by its almost black bark and long, perpendicular spines.

FRUITS: The spherical stone fruits ④ are the size of a Bilberry and have a dark-blue skin, with a slight whitish tinge.

DISTRIBUTION: On woodland edges, in coppices and meadow hedges, and on dry river banks; also commonly planted to divide fields and meadows.

OTHER: The Blackthorn is edible, but very sour. After the first frosts, the taste becomes milder.

129

Alder Buckthorn

Frangula alnus

DESCRIPTION: The Alder Buckthorn is deciduous and can grow either as a shrub or a small tree, reaching a height of about 3m ①. It never has thorns. The dark red-brown, smooth bark has noticeable, wart-like flecks ②.

LEAVES: The stemmed leaves are oval, but end in a point. Their edges are smooth and slightly waved.

BLOOMS: The plain, green-white flowers ③ are found individually or in small groups where the leaf stem joins the branch. Each flower has five sepals and five petals.

TYPICAL FEATURES

The Common Buckthorn (p86) is very similar, but the Alder Buckthorn can be distinguished by its alternating leaves and its lack of spines.

FRUITS: The spherical stone fruits are about 8mm in diameter ④ and change in colour from green to red to a purple-black.

DISTRIBUTION: On woodland trails and woodland edges, in lowland coppices and mixed conifer woodland; only found in wet soil.

OTHER: All parts of the Alder Buckthorn contain powerful poisons.

Purple Willow

Salix purpurea

DESCRIPTION: The Purple Willow is a deciduous shrub, which can grow to a height of 6m ①. It sometimes also grows to form a small tree. Its branches are flexible, grow straight upwards and have many smaller branches.

LEAVES: The long, narrow leaves form a point at the tips ②. Both the upper surface of the leaves and the underside have no hairs. The underside is a blue-green colour. The leaf edge is normally only serrated at the tip.

TYPICAL FEATURES

Young Purple Willow branches are usually a bright red colour, especially those that receive most sunlight.

BLOOMS: The flowers often appear just before or at the same time as the leaves. Male and female catkins are found on different plants. Shortly after blooming, the male catkins are a bright red ③, but before blooming they are a greenish-yellow colour ④.

FRUITS: The capsules ripen by early summer and release numerous hairy seeds, which cling together like cotton wool.

DISTRIBUTION: On riverbanks and in lowland forests.

OTHER: The flexible branches were once used for basket-making.

Goat Willow

Salix caprea

DESCRIPTION: Goat Willow is deciduous and grows to form a shrub of around 3m, or a tree of around 12m in height ①. Young branches have a small number of hairs; older branches have none. Young plants have a smooth, grey bark, but this later forms long cracks.

LEAVES: The stemmed leaves ② are oval and end in a short point, which is often slightly curved. The leaf edge is smooth, and has only slight serration, if any.

TYPICAL FEATURES
The leaves of the Goat Willow have felt-like hairs on the underside. The underside of the leaf also has prominent leaf veins.

BLOOMS: Flowers appear in spring before the leaves; male and female flowers appear on different plants. When immature ③, the catkins are covered in a soft, silvery fur. When in full bloom, these are yellow ① and about 3cm long.

FRUITS: The ripe capsules burst open and and release large numbers of hairy seeds ④, which are dispersed by the wind.

DISTRIBUTION: Woodland edges, fallow land, gravel pits and quarries.

Grey Willow | Grey Sallow

Salix cinerea

DESCRIPTION: The deciduous Grey Willow is a 3m-high shrub ①, but it can also grow to form a small tree. It has dark green, hair-covered branches. All of the main branches are of about the same length, giving the crown a flat appearance.

LEAVES: The stemmed, oval leaves end in a point. The edges have a regular, fine serration, or are smooth. They have grey, velvety hairs, particularly on the underside ②. The under-side of the leaves also has prominent veins.

TYPICAL FEATURES
Young Grey Willow branches have grey felt-like hairs. The oblong buds, located where the leaf stem joins the branch, are a uniform white ③.

BLOOMS: As with all willows, the flowers form in catkins, with male and female flowers on different plants. Male catkins ④ are 5cm long and are slightly smaller than the female ones; the stamen are initially red, but later turn yellow.

FRUITS: The unremarkable capsule fruits release numerous seeds with white hairs when ripe.

DISTRIBUTION: Ditches, bogs, banks, moorland edges and marshes.

133

Snowy Mespilus

Amelanchier ovalis

DESCRIPTION: The Snowy Mespilus is a deciduous shrub, about 1–3m tall, with much-forked branches and a dense crown ①. The main branches are quite thin. Young branches have felt-like hairs; these later disappear to reveal an olive-brown bark.

LEAVES: The stemmed, round to oval leaves have fine serration along the edges ②.

BLOOMS: The white flowers appear before the leaves. They are positioned at the ends of the branches in panicles. The individual flowers have five narrow petals ③.

TYPICAL FEATURES

When they first emerge, the leaves of the Snowy Mespilus have a yellowish, hairy underside. Older leaves only have hairs along the leaf veins.

FRUITS: The pea-sized apple fruits are initially green to red, but turn blue-black with a light tinge ④.

DISTRIBUTION: In cliff-top coppices, rocky outcrops and dry meadows.

OTHER: The numerous fruits are edible and full of flavour.

Mahaleb Cherry

Prunus mahaleb

DESCRIPTION: The Mahaleb Cherry is a deciduous shrub, 1–3 metres high, with loose branches and many twigs ①. It can sometimes also grow to form a small tree with several trunks and a broad crown.

LEAVES: The stemmed, round to oval leaves have a small point at the tip ②. The edge is slightly serrated. The veins on the underside of the leaf carry hairs.

BLOOMS: The pure white flowers have a pleasant aroma and are arranged in multi-stemmed

TYPICAL FEATURES

Young Mahaleb Cherry branches have fine hairs and are sticky to the touch. Small pores are visible on the bark.

racemes ③. The individual flowers have five petals with rounded tips.

FRUITS: In mid-summer, pea-sized stone fruits form in bunches. As they ripen, their colour changes from red to black ④.

DISTRIBUTION: In coppices at the foot of cliffs; in light deciduous woodland; on dry, sunny outcrops; very often found in wine-growing regions.

OTHER: The fruits are edible, but do not taste good. The stone is used in Greek cookery as a flavouring.

135

Holly
Ilex aquifolium

DESCRIPTION: The evergreen Holly is a shrub with very dense foliage, which can reach a height of 1–5m. It can also occasionally grow to form a 10m-high tree.

LEAVES: The shiny leaves feel stiff and leathery. Most have a thorny serration ②; smooth-edged leaves are less common ③.

BLOOMS: The small flowers have four and occasionally five petals ④. The flowers form in clusters where the leaf joins the branch. Male and female flowers form on different plants.

TYPICAL FEATURES
Smooth-edged and spiky leaves can form on the same plants. There can also be several types of intermediate leaf shape.

FRUITS: Roughly pea-sized, bright red stone fruits ① form on the female plants. They remain on the branches into the winter.

DISTRIBUTION: Light deciduous woodland, coppices; common in low mountain ranges and grown as an ornamental plant.

OTHER: The leaves and fruits of the Holly are poisonous. Very popular as a Christmas decoration.

Sea Buckthorn
Hippophae rhamnoides

DESCRIPTION: Sea Buckthorn is a deciduous shrub, which can grow to a height of 2–3m ① and can sometimes also grow to form a small tree. In tree form it can reach a height of 10m. Its branches have long spines ③, which develop from small twigs.

LEAVES: The leaves are long and very narrow ②. The top of the leaf is a grey-green colour, but the underside has a silvery shimmer.

TYPICAL FEATURES
The Sea Buckthorn can be easily identified by its spiny branches and narrow, silvery leaves.

BLOOMS: The flowers form before the leaves. They are only a few millimetres long and are unremarkable. Male and female flowers form on different plants.

FRUITS: The bright orange fruits form in dense fruit clusters ④. They are berry-like and contain a stone seed.

DISTRIBUTION: On gravel banks near water, in coastal dunes.

OTHER: The fruit of the Sea Buckthorn is rich in Vitamin C and is edible. When uncooked, the fruits are sour, and they are often made into a juice.

Midland Hawthorn
May Hawthorn
Crataegus laevigata

DESCRIPTION: The Midland Hawthorn grows either as a 2–5m-high shrub ① or as a tree up to 10m tall. Young branches are red-brown but turn grey with age. The smaller branches have spines up to 1.5cm long.

LEAVES: The small, stemmed, broad oval leaves have three, and occasionally five, rounded lobes ②, and irregular serration.

BLOOMS: Numerous white flowers ④ are arranged as umbellate panicles. They have a strong, unpleasant aroma, five petals, numerous red stamen and are 1–1.5cm wide.

FRUITS: The scarlet-red haws have a diameter of about 1cm ③ and still carry the petals as a form of 'crown'.

DISTRIBUTION: At the edges of woods, in coppices and hedgerows; often also planted as ornamentals and often found growing with wild roses.

> **TYPICAL FEATURES**
> The best method of distinguishing the Midland Hawthorn from the Common Hawthorn is by identifying its double style in the flower.

Common Hawthorn
Crataegus monogyna

DESCRIPTION: The Common Hawthorn is a deciduous plant, growing either as a 3–5m-high shrub ① or a tree up to 8m tall. Branches have a dense covering of smaller branches and form an almost impenetrable mass. The branches carry fierce spines up to 1cm long ③.

LEAVES: The long stemmed, oval leaves are up to 8cm long and and are divided into between three and seven clearly defined lobes ②. The leaves have a tough texture. The veins on the underside of the leaves carry tufts of hairs.

BLOOMS: The white flowers have five petals and form in dense, upright, umbellate panicles at the ends of the branches. They have a strong, unpleasant aroma, slightly reminiscent of fish.

FRUITS: The shiny scarlet red, spherical haws ④ have a diameter of about 1cm.

DISTRIBUTION: In light woodland, on woodland edges, in coppices; often also planted in parks and gardens.

> **TYPICAL FEATURES**
> The flowers of the Common Hawthorn only have one style, and the fruits only contain a single seed.

Quince
Cydonia oblonga

DESCRIPTION: The Quince grows to form a shrub of up to 5m in height ① or a small tree. It has long, stiff branches, and young side-branches have dense, felt-like hairs.

LEAVES: The oval, normally slightly wavy leaves ② have a smooth edge.

BLOOMS: Bowl-shaped flowers have a white to light pink colouring ③ and form individually or in pairs at the ends of the side branches.

FRUITS: The fruit of the Quince ④ has the same form as an apple or pear. On cultivated specimens, the fruits can also grow to a similar size. They have a thick, downy covering and are light yellow when ripe.

TYPICAL FEATURES
The five-petalled flowers of the Quince have a 4–6cm diameter, making them conspicuously large. The underside of the leaves have dense, felt-like hairs.

DISTRIBUTION: Native to south-east Europe and the Near East; in Central Europe it is grown as a fruit tree.

OTHER: The fruit of the Quince can only be eaten cooked. They can be cooked and sweetened to make juice, jams or jelly.

Medlar
Mespilus germanica

DESCRIPTION: The Medlar is deciduous and can grow to a height of 2–5m, either as a shrub or in tree form ①. The branches form a broad crown. They sometimes have spines and new growth carries grey, felt-like hairs.

LEAVES: The stemmed leaves are up to 12cm long. They are a long, oval shape and have a smooth edge ②. In autumn the leaves turn a bright yellow colour.

BLOOMS: The flowers are up to 5cm in size ③ and form individually at the ends of the branches. The narrow sepals are visible between the five white petals.

TYPICAL FEATURES
The long, wrinkled leaves of the Medlar have hairs on the underside. Where the leaf-stem joins the branch, there are two short stipules.

FRUITS: The spherical, 2–3cm wide fruits ④ are covered in hairs and feel hard. The remains of the sepals are still visible.

DISTRIBUTION: Originally from south-east Europe and the Near East; introduced to England in the Middle Ages, but now rare.

OTHER: The fruits of the Medlar are only edible when overripe and cooked.

Hazel | Hazelnut
Corylus avellana

DESCRIPTION: The Hazel is deciduous and can either grow as a 2–4m-high, broad shrub ①, or occasionally as a tree up to 6m tall. It is recognisable by the large number of straight, young branches, which grow each year from the rootstock.

LEAVES: The short-stemmed leaves ② have a round contour and end in short point. The edges are rough with fine serration.

BLOOMS: The flowers ③ appear long before the leaves. The male catkins hang limply from the branches; the female clusters are small and bud-shaped, and the stigma have an intense red colour.

FRUITS: The nuts are located individually or in groups on the branches ④.

DISTRIBUTION: Woodland edges, coppices, hedgerows and river banks.

OTHER: Hazelnuts have a high protein and oil content.

TYPICAL FEATURES
The Hazel can be easily identified by its typical leaf shape and nuts, which grow within a bowl of shredded leaf-like coverings.

Turkish Hazel | Tree Hazel
Corylus colurna

DESCRIPTION: The Turkish Hazel is a deciduous tree, growing to a height of up to 20m ①. It has a straight trunk and a tapering crown. Older plants have a grey bark, which flakes off in pieces.

LEAVES: The long-stemmed leaves hang down slightly and are round to oval, ending in a point ②. They have an irregular edge, sometimes with fine serration.

BLOOMS: Male flowers form in long, hanging catkins; female flowers grow in small, bud-like clusters ③.

TYPICAL FEATURES
The Turkish Hazel has larger leaves than the Hazel, and the stems have sticky hairs. The tough fruit casing also feels sticky.

FRUITS: The nuts form in dense clumps ④. They are completely surrounded by a casing, with long, shredded tufts.

DISTRIBUTION: South-east Europe, western Asia; introduced into the United Kingdom as a park tree.

OTHER: Hazelnuts sold commmercially do not generally come from the European Hazel, but from the Turkish Hazel.

143

Basket Willow | Common Osier
Salix viminalis

DESCRIPTION: The Basket Willow is deciduous and grows either as a 10m-high tree or a dense shrub. The vertical branches are initially covered with velvety, grey hairs, but become green and hairless with age. The bark on old branches has deep, lengthwise cracks.

LEAVES: The very narrow leaves ② can grow to about 20cm long. The edges curve slightly under, and the underside has silver hairs.

BLOOMS: The flowers appear before the leaves and form in catkins ③. Male and female flowers form on different plants.

TYPICAL FEATURES
When the Basket Willow is pruned back it forms long, rod-shaped branches ①. This process is called pollarding.

FRUITS: The inconspicuous capsule fruits burst open when ripe and release numerous seeds with fluffy, white flight hairs.

DISTRIBUTION: Meadows, banks, ditches; often planted in sandy soil.

OTHER: The Basket Willow used to be pruned back dramatically ④ and the long, thin branches were used to weave baskets.

Hoary Willow
Salix elaeagnos

DESCRIPTION: The Hoary Willow is a shrub that can reach a height of 3–6m ①. If growing in free space, some plants can sometimes also grow to form a small tree.

LEAVES: The short-stemmed, very narrow leaves grow to a length of 15cm. The edges curve slightly under and the leaf tip has slight serration. The hairs on the underside of the leaves are grey and felt-like.

BLOOMS: Male and female catkins form shortly before or at the same time as the leaves. They are found on different plants. The female catkins are 6cm long, about double the length of the male catkins ②.

TYPICAL FEATURES
Narrow leaves, with felt-like, matte hairs, are characteristic of the Hoary Willow. In winter, bright red buds become apparent ③.

FRUITS: The capsules release numerous white-haired seeds. These often clump together in a woolly ball ④.

DISTRIBUTION: In mountain ranges above the tree line and in gravel pits near water.

145

Almond Tree
Prunus dulcis

DESCRIPTION: The Almond Tree can reach a height of 10m and has a broad, loose crown with upward growing branches ①.
LEAVES: The stemmed, long oval leaves ② end in a long point. The edges have a fine serration.
BLOOMS: The white to bright pink coloured flowers ④ form individually or, more commonly, in pairs on short stems. They appear very early in the year, before the leaves emerge.

TYPICAL FEATURES

The older branches on the Almond Tree have an almost black bark, which flakes off in small patches.

FRUITS: The egg-shaped, grey-green, hairy stone-fruits are up to 4cm long ③. When ripe, the dry fruit flesh bursts open and reveals the stone kernel, with an edible seed, the sweet almond.
DISTRIBUTION: From North Africa to Syria; only found in Central Europe in regions with a favourable climate, for example in wine-growing areas.
OTHER: The Bitter Almond (*Prunus dulcis* var. *amara*) is a variety whose seeds are rich in hydrocyanic acid.

Garden Plum | Damson
Prunus domestica

DESCRIPTION: Deciduous tree, up to 10–15m high, with a straight trunk and an irregularly shaped crown ①. Wild plants sometimes form spines, but cultivated plants do not.
LEAVES: Stemmed and oval, with finely serrated edges ②. Undersides are slightly hairy.
BLOOMS: Pure white, five-petalled flowers ③ appear in spring at about the same time as the leaves. They sometimes form individually, but are more common in pairs or in threes at the ends of the smaller branches.

TYPICAL FEATURES

Younger branches are covered in hairs. The undersides of the leaves are lighter than the upper surfaces and are also hairy.

FRUITS: In wild varieties the well-known, juicy stone-fruits or drupes are dark violet in colour with a glaucous blue sheen ④.
DISTRIBUTION: Native to Asia Minor; in the United Kingdom, there are many varieties of Garden Plum.
OTHER: The Garden Plum is a very old cultivated plant. Some varieties crossed over the Alps into northern Europe with the Romans. Greengages, Damsons and Mirabelles are sub-species of the Garden Plum.

147

Wild Crab | Wild Apple Tree

Malus sylvestris

DESCRIPTION: Deciduous tree, reaching a height of about 10m with a broad crown. Also grows in shrub form ①. Branches have many smaller branches and sometimes have spines.

LEAVES: Stemmed leaves are oval to almost round ②. Edges have slight serration. Young leaves have hairs on both sides, but older leaves have hairs only on the veins.

BLOOMS: Flowers arranged in small numbers on umbellate racemes at the ends of the branches. Outer surface of the petals is pink, and the inside is white ③.

TYPICAL FEATURES
The Wild Crab can be hard to identify. It can, however, be easily distinguished when in fruit.

FRUITS: The apples are only slightly succulent and have a diameter of only 2–3cm. They have a hard, sour-flavoured flesh.

DISTRIBUTION: Deciduous and mixed woodland, lowland woodland, hedgerows and coppices.

OTHER: The Wild Crab and other wild species have been bred to produce more that a thousand species of cultivated apple ④.

Wild Pear

Pyrus pyraster

DESCRIPTION: The Wild Pear is deciduous and can grow either as a 2–4m-high shrub ① or as a tree up to 20m tall.

LEAVES: The leaf stem is at least as long as the width of the leaf. The rounded leaves have smooth edges or a fine serration. Young leaves have dense hairs on both sides; older leaves only have hairs on the underside.

BLOOMS: White flowers ② are found in small numbers on umbellate racemes on the smaller

TYPICAL FEATURES
Small, long-stemmed leaves and powerful spines ④ at the branch tips are characteristic of the Wild Pear.

branches. Each flower has five petals and numerous wine-red stamen.

FRUITS: Fruits are 4–5cm long and are noticeably smaller than cultivated pears. They have a red to yellow colour ③ and are edible, but very hard.

DISTRIBUTION: In coppices, hedgerows and light woodland; rare, and only ever found individually.

OTHER: The Wild Pear is one of the original plants from which the cultivated Garden Pear was bred. Garden Pears are larger and have a greater sugar content – the small Wild Pears have a sour flavour.

Whitebeam
Sorbus aria

DESCRIPTION: The Whitebeam is a deciduous tree which can grow to a height of 15m. It has a straight trunk and a round crown ①. It can also grow as a shrub with vertical branches. Young branches have grey, felt-like hairs. The trunks of older trees have a grey, cracked bark.

LEAVES: The oval leaves have slightly serrated edges. The leaf-stem and the underside of the leaves ③ have dense, grey-white, felt-like hairs. In autumn the foliage turns a yellow-red.

TYPICAL FEATURES
The Whitebeam has characteristic grey-white hairs on the young branches, leaves and flower stems.

BLOOMS: The numerous white, five-petalled flowers ② form in large, umbrella-shaped panicles at the ends of the branches. Flower stems and sepals have felt-like hairs.

FRUITS: Spherical apple fruits with a diameter of 1cm ④; bright coral-red.

DISTRIBUTION: On sunny slopes, in deciduous and pine woodland in Central Europe. Ornamental in the United Kingdom.

OTHER: The fruits are edible, but have no flavour.

Wild Service Tree
Sorbus torminalis

DESCRIPTION: The deciduous Wild Service Tree normally grows as a 20m-high tree with an egg-shaped crown, but can sometimes also form a small shrub ①. Young bark is smooth and grey, but becomes dark brown on older branches and falls away in small flakes.

LEAVES: The long-stemmed leaves ④ come in a range of sizes, with pointed lobes. Each lobe has a serrated edge. In autumn the foliage turns a bright orange-red.

TYPICAL FEATURES
The shape of the leaves is very similar to that of the Maple, but the leaves of the Wild Service Tree are alternating.

BLOOMS: White flowers ② have stems covered in felt-like stems and form in vertical, umbrella-like, broad panicles.

FRUITS: The long apple fruits ③ are slightly smaller than grapes, and have a red to light brown colour with fine white speckling.

DISTRIBUTION: Sunny slopes, mixed woodland; often in wine-growing regions.

OTHER: The mealy fruits used to be used as finings during must production, due to their high tannic acid content.

151

Bird Cherry
Prunus padus

DESCRIPTION: The Bird Cherry is a deciduous tree, with multiple trunks, which can grow to a height of 18m ①. They sometimes do not grow very tall and instead form shrubs with upright branches. Light brown, wart-like markings can be seen on the younger branches. The main branches and the trunk have a dark brown to almost black bark.

TYPICAL FEATURES
Characteristic features of the Bird Cherry are hanging racemes or racemes which curve downwards.

LEAVES: Oval leaves have fine serration along the edges ② and end in a point. The veins on the leaf surface curve and join up before reaching the leaf edge.

BLOOMS: White, aromatic flowers form in 15cm-long hanging racemes ④. Individual flowers consist of five sepals, which fall off early, and five petals.

FRUITS: When ripe, the pea-sized stone fruits are shiny black ③.

DISTRIBUTION: Lowland forests, damp river banks and deciduous woodland.

OTHER: The seeds are poisonous when raw.

Black Cherry
Prunus serotina

DESCRIPTION: The Black Cherry is a deciduous tree, which can reach a height of 30m. It has a broad, irregular crown. It often grows with several main trunks with an aromatic, fissured bark ②.

TYPICAL FEATURES
The flower racemes of the Black Cherry form either upright or angling upwards, but never hang beneath the branch.

LEAVES: The stemmed, oval leaves ① end in a short point and have a slightly wavy edge. The undersides are slightly lighter than the upper surface of the leaf, and the central vein has white or orange-coloured hairs.

BLOOMS: The white flowers are arranged in 10–15cm long racemes ③. The individual flowers have five petals and five short sepals.

FRUITS: The spherical stone fruits have a diameter of about 1cm and change in colour from red to almost black when ripe ④.

DISTRIBUTION: Native to North America; grown in Central Europe as park or street shrubbery and has become wild in some places.

OTHER: The fruit seeds should not be consumed uncooked.

153

Wild Cherry
Prunus avium

DESCRIPTION: A deciduous tree, which can grow to a height of 30m and has a very regular, tapering or round crown ①. Older trunks have smooth bark with horizontal, wart-like stripes ②. The bark rolls up in horizontal strips.

LEAVES: Stemmed, oval leaves end in a short point ③. Edges have forward-pointing serration.

BLOOMS: Five-petalled flowers arranged in groups of two to five on shorter branches.

FRUITS: Cherries hang from branches on long stems ④ and change colour from yellow, to red, to almost black when ripe.

DISTRIBUTION: Deciduous and mixed woodland, but also woodland edges and hedgerows.

OTHER: Cultivated sweet cherries originate from the Wild Cherry. Its fruits are edible, but are slightly bitter. Unlike the Bird Cherry (p152), the seeds do not contain hydrocyanic acid.

TYPICAL FEATURES
The veins on the underside of the leaf have a light covering of hairs, and there are two red pores on the leaf stems.

White Oak | Downy Oak
Quercus pubescens

DESCRIPTION: The White Oak is a deciduous tree reaching a height of 25m, or it can grow as a shrub. Grows with several main trunks and older trees have a crooked, gnarled appearance ① with a thick and heavily fissured bark ②.

LEAVES: The leaves have rounded lobes ④ with egg-shaped contours. The leaves become narrower nearer the stem. Young leaves have dense hairs on both sides, but older leaves have hairs on the underside alone.

BLOOMS: The flowers emerge in spring at the same time as the leaves. The male flowers hang in narrow, yellow catkins, while the female flowers are tiny and unremarkable.

FRUITS: The acorns ③ ripen in short-stemmed fruit clusters. Up to a third of the acorn is covered by a tight cup, covered in grey, felt-like hairs.

DISTRIBUTION: Southern Europe, southern regions of Central and Western Europe, Asia Minor; in more northern parts it is only found on sunny slopes in wine-growing regions.

TYPICAL FEATURES
The best way to identify the White Oak is by its densely haired young branches, leaf-stems and undersides of the leaves.

Common Ivy
Hedera helix

DESCRIPTION: The Common Ivy is an evergreen climbing shrub, which can climb to a height of 20m with suitable support.

LEAVES: The stemmed, slightly leathery leaves have between three and five lobes, if growing on non-flowering branches ①. Flowering branches have oval or diamond-shaped leaves with smooth edges ②. The surfaces of the leaf have a light and dark-green patterning.

BLOOMS: The yellow flowers first open in autumn. The greenish individual flowers are unremarkable, but form in groups in conspicuous, semi-spherical umbels ④.

FRUITS: The spherical, black berries ripen in February the following year ③, and remain on the branches for a long time. The former style protrudes from the flat tip of the fruit.

DISTRIBUTION: Shady woodland, coppices, meadows, walls and buildings.

OTHER: All parts of the Common Ivy are poisonous.

Grape Vine
Vitis vinifera

DESCRIPTION: The Grape Vine is a deciduous climbing shrub, which can grow to a height of 20m using its gripping shoots. Cultivated varieties are regularly pruned and therefore remain smaller. The grey-brown bark flakes in thin strips.

LEAVES: The long-stemmed leaves have a round contour, but have three to five well-defined lobes ②. The underside of the leaf has hairs and the edges have a marked serration.

BLOOMS: The small green flowers form in vertical panicles ③. In wild varieties, male and female flowers form on different plants, but cultivated plants carry both flowers.

FRUITS: In wild varieties, blue grapes grow in hanging panicles and only reach the size of a pea. The grapes on cultivated vines are normally bigger and depending on the variety are green-yellow ④, red-brown or blue ①.

DISTRIBUTION: In lowland forests, mainly in the Mediterranean, otherwise very rare; cultivated varieties grow in sunny regions with a warm climate.

Common Alder | Black Alder
Alnus glutinosa

DESCRIPTION: The Common Alder is a deciduous tree, which can grow to a height of 30m ①. It has a straight, high-reaching trunk and an oval crown. Young branches have a shiny, reddish to green bark; larger branches and the trunk have a very dark, almost black bark.

LEAVES: The round leaves are often slightly lobed at the tip ②. The edges are serrated, and the veins on the underside of the leaves have hairs.

BLOOMS: The flowers appear before the leaves. Male flowers hang in catkins from the branches; the female flowers are small, cone-like clusters.

FRUITS: In autumn, the female flower clusters ripen into woody cones ③ and then release small, winged nuts.

DISTRIBUTION: Pond and river banks, lowland forests; in damp to wet soil; also often used to reinforce the banks of natural streams and brooks ④.

Grey Alder
Alnus incana

DESCRIPTION: The Grey Alder is a tree, which can reach a height of 15m. It has several main trunks and a rounded crown ①. It has a smooth, silver-grey bark ②.

LEAVES: The oval, often pointed leaves have indented edges, which in turn are finely serrated ④. The slightly lighter, bluish undersides have dense hairs when young, but fully developed leaves only have hairs on the veins.

BLOOMS: The flowers appear long before the leaves. The male flowers form narrow catkins, which hang limply from the branches; the small female flowers are cone-like and have a red colour ③.

FRUITS: In autumn, the woody cones ripen and release thin, winged nut fruits, which are then distributed by the wind.

DISTRIBUTION: In lowland forests, on river and pond banks; mainly in low mountain ranges.

159

White Willow

Salix alba

DESCRIPTION: The White Willow is a deciduous tree, which can grow to a height of 25m ①. It has a thick trunk and vertical main branches. The red-brown, young branches have close-lying hairs. Older trees have branches with rough bark and net-like fissures ②.

TYPICAL FEATURES
The silver-white underside of the narrow leaves is a characteristic feature, giving the tree its name.

LEAVES: The long, narrow leaves are about 10cm long ④ and end in a point. The leaf edges are finely serrated.

BLOOMS: Male and female flowers form on different plants. The yellow male catkins ③ can be up to 7cm long, and the female green catkins can be up to 5cm long.

FRUITS: The tiny capsule fruits ripen as early as late spring. They release large numbers of seeds with white flight hairs.

DISTRIBUTION: On the banks of flowing waterways, particularly in areas that are frequently flooded.

Crack Willow

Salix fragilis

DESCRIPTION: The Crack Willow is a deciduous tree, growing to a height of 15m ①, but it can also grow in shrub form. It has a loose, irregular crown with very long, thin branches, which are a shiny, yellow to brown colour.

TYPICAL FEATURES
If you snap a young Crack Willow branch, it breaks away with a very loud 'crack'.

LEAVES: The stemmed, narrow, oval leaves have a long point and finely serrated edges ②. The underside of the leaf is slightly lighter than the shiny upper surface.

BLOOMS: The flowers appear before the leaves. Male and female flowers are found on different plants. The female catkins ④ hang on long stems from the branches; the male catkins ③ are smaller, and their buds have a white layer of hair.

FRUITS: The tiny capsule fruits contain many seeds with white flight hairs, which clump together in a bundle.

DISTRIBUTION: In river and pondside fields; on damp soil that does not contain limestone. Mainly in low-lying areas and in mountain valleys.

161

Ginkgo biloba | Maiden Hair Tree
Ginkgo biloba

DESCRIPTION: Gingko biloba is a deciduous tree, which can reach a height of 30m. It has an irregular crown ①.

LEAVES: Long-stemmed leaves grow in clusters on the smaller branches ④. They have a conspicuous fan-shape, often with an indent between the two halves. Leaf veins also form a fan-shape.

BLOOMS: The yellow, male catkins ② and the female seed pods appear on different plants at the same time as the leaves.

FRUITS: In autumn, the yellow, mirabelle-like fruits ripen ③. They are spherical, with a diameter of about 2–3cm, and hang individually or in pairs on long stems from the branches.

DISTRIBUTION: South-east China. Grown in the United Kingdom as an ornamental and park plant.

OTHER: Gingko biloba is a living fossil. The only related species are 100 million-year-old fossils.

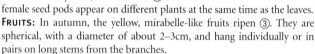

Hornbeam
Carpinus betulus

DESCRIPTION: A deciduous tree, which can reach a height of about 25m ①. It has a rounded crown and the trunk has smooth, grey bark, with a raised, criss-cross patterning ②.

LEAVES: The stemmed, oval leaves end in a point ③. The leaf edge has indentations, which in turn have fine serration.

BLOOMS: The flower catkins appear in spring at the same time as the leaves. The male catkins are up to 7cm long and hang limply from the branches; the female catkins are only 2cm long and are located on the branch tips, surrounded by pale green leaves.

FRUITS: Light green fruits ④ hang in bushy clusters from the branches in autumn. Each of the small, oval nut fruits has a three-lobed wing, which helps the seeds to 'fly' and disperse.

DISTRIBUTION: In deciduous woodland, near footpaths; as a garden hedge.

OTHER: Hornbeam wood is particularly heavy and hard, and used to be used mainly for making tools.

Silver Birch
Betula pendula

DESCRIPTION: The Silver birch is a deciduous tree which can reach a height of 30m. It has an oval crown, with hanging branches ①. The bark on the trunk is white, but interspersed with large, black patches ②.

LEAVES: The stemmed, round to triangular leaves end in a point ③. The edges are indented and finely serrated. In autumn, the foliage turns a golden yellow.

TYPICAL FEATURES
The black and white bark and the hanging branches make the Silver Birch unmistakable.

BLOOMS: The flowers appear in spring at the same time as the leaves. The long, yellow-green male catkins hang at the ends of the older branches; the cone-like female flowers initially stand upright on the smaller branches, but later hang downwards.

FRUITS: Tiny, green, winged nuts form in dense, hanging clusters ④.

DISTRIBUTION: Woodland edges, coppices, heathland, moors, fallow land.

Downy Birch
Betula pubescens

DESCRIPTION: A deciduous tree, which can grow to 20m tall ①. It has an oval crown. The bark on the trunk and main branches is white and flakes away in horizontal strips ③.

LEAVES: The stemmed leaves are more egg-shaped than diamond-shaped ④. Young leaves have hairs; fully developed leaves are hairless, apart from small tufts of hair on the leaf veins on the underside of the leaf.

TYPICAL FEATURES
The branches of the Downy Birch angle steeply upwards and never hang down.

BLOOMS: Flowers appear at the same time as the leaves. Yellow male catkins ② hang limply beneath the branches; the short, cone-like female flowers are light green and stand vertically.

FRUITS: Dense fruit clusters develop from the female flower and hang from the branches ④, becoming brown when ripe. They then release tiny seeds with two narrow wings.

DISTRIBUTION: In moors, damp woods and water-meadows.

OTHER: The Silver and Downy Birch can cross-pollinate. The resulting plants display characteristics of both parents.

165

Common Beech
Fagus sylvatica

DESCRIPTION: The Common Beech is a deciduous tree which can grow to a height of 40m ①. In woods it forms a single, straight trunk with a smooth, grey bark ②. Lone plants have a shorter trunk and a broader crown.

LEAVES: The stemmed, oval leaves have a short, pointed tip ③. Young leaves have hairs at the edges; older leaves have a smooth edge or slight serration. Autumn foliage is a bright yellow or brown.

TYPICAL FEATURES
The open fruit cups and the shiny, three-edged beechnuts make the Common Beech easy to identify.

BLOOMS: The unremarkable flowers appear at the same time as the leaves. Male flowers hang in stemmed clumps beneath the branch; female flowers stand upright in green cups with felt-like hairs.

FRUITS: The angular, brown nuts (beechnuts) form in woody, spiky cups, which open into four flaps ④. The ground cover from them is known as beech mast.

DISTRIBUTION: In deciduous woodland; on limestone.

Red Oak
Quercus rubra

DESCRIPTION: The Red Oak is a deciduous tree, which can reach a height of 30–40m. Young trees have a tapering crown, but more established plants have a broad, reaching crown ①. Young branches have a reddish bark with lighter spots. Trunk has a dark grey bark ②.

LEAVES: The leaves are divided into pointed lobes ④. The indentations between the lobes extend halfway to the leaf spine. Small tufts of hairs grow on the leaf veins on the underside of the leaf. In autumn, the foliage turns a bright carmine or vermillion red.

TYPICAL FEATURES
The leaf veins on the leaves of the Red Oak run to the very tips of the lobes and end in a short point.

BLOOMS: Male catkins hang far below the branches; the very unremarkable female flowers are located at the branch tips.

FRUITS: The short-stemmed acorns ③ are about 2.5cm long and sit in a very flat cup. They do not become ripe until their second year.

DISTRIBUTION: Native to eastern parts of North America; introduced to Central Europe as early as the 17th century as an ornamental, park plant.

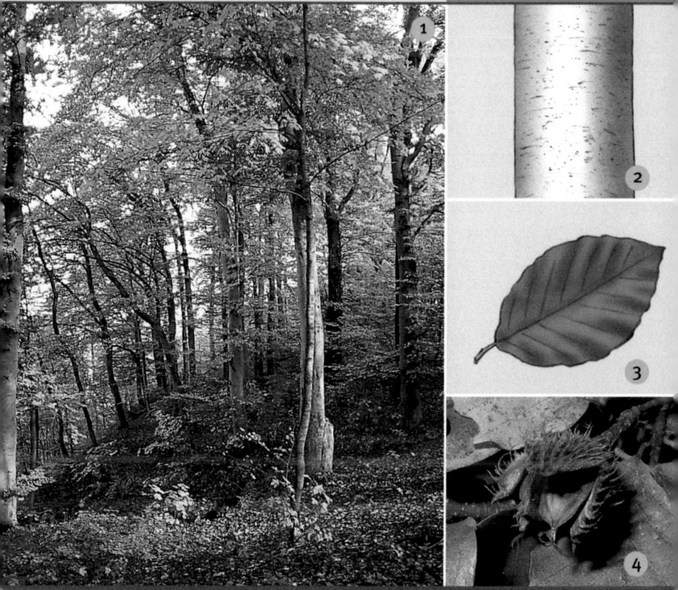
1
2
3
4

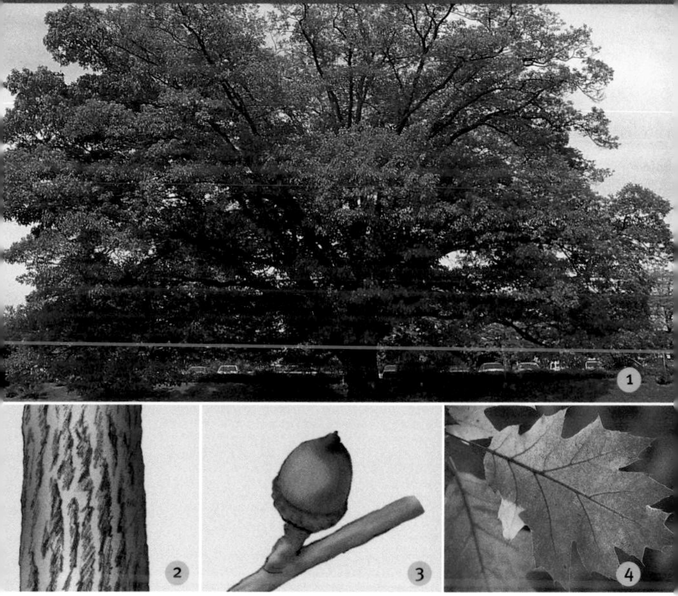
1
2
3
4

Magnolia
Magnolia x *soulangiana*

DESCRIPTION: A deciduous shrub reaching a height of 2–3m ①; some can reach a height of up to 8m. Forms a dense, round crown.

LEAVES: The long oval leaves ② have a prominent short point and a smooth, sometimes slightly wavy, edge.

BLOOMS: The large flowers ③ emerge before the leaves from thick buds covered in a skin of dense hairs. The white petals curve slightly outwards and have a pink colour on the outer surface. The petals form tulip-shaped blooms, which later open out and become flat.

FRUITS: Long, woody pods form in mid-summer, but only during warm years. The seeds develop within these pods. The seeds have a bright, light red coating ④.

DISTRIBUTION: Native to woodland areas of eastern Asia; introduced to Central Europe as an ornamental shrub, but does not grow wild.

TYPICAL FEATURES

Magnolias are unmistakable when in bloom, due to their very large flowers, forming on bare branches ①.

Tulip Tree | Yellow Poplar
Liriodendron tulipifera

DESCRIPTION: The Tulip Tree is deciduous and can reach a height of up to 35m ①. It has a straight trunk, and well-established plants form a cloud-shaped crown.

LEAVES: The long-stemmed leaves can be up to 20cm long and almost the same width ③; the end of the leaf is divided into two lobes and looks as though the tip has been cut off. Near the stem there are two further lobes, which stand out almost at right angles.

TYPICAL FEATURES

Outside the blooming period, the Tulip Tree can be identified by its winged fruits and unusual leaves.

BLOOMS: The conspicuously large, tulip-shaped flowers ④ appear in late spring from egg-shaped buds. They consist of six greenish-yellow petals, which are orange at the base. The petals surround numerous pale yellow stamen.

FRUITS: The cone-shaped fruits ② form upright on the branches. They consist of small, winged nuts.

DISTRIBUTION: Native to eastern parts of North America; introduced to Central Europe as an ornamental park plant.

169

Aspen | Trembling Poplar
Populus tremula

DESCRIPTION: The Aspen is a deciduous tree, which can reach a height of 30m and which has a loose, lightly branched crown ①. The lower branches are normally horizontal. The bark is initially smooth and grey-brown ② but becomes almost black with long fissures as the tree ages.

LEAVES: The round leaves have blunt serrated edges ④. Older branches have larger leaves with short stems.

BLOOMS: Male and female catkins ③ – both a red-yellow colour – appear on different plants.

FRUITS: Consist of pods with two sides, which release small seeds with flight hairs in late spring.

DISTRIBUTION: On deforested areas, on woodland edges and near footpaths, in gravel pits, quarries and rocky areas.

TYPICAL FEATURES
The Aspen's round leaves hang vertically down from leaf-stems, which are almost at right angles to the leaf. Even in light winds, the leaves rustle loudly.

Grey Poplar
Populus x canescens

DESCRIPTION: The Grey Poplar is a deciduous tree, which can reach a height of 35m ①. Its powerful trunk has a dark, grey-brown bark ② and divides into several, vertical branches.

LEAVES: The leaves can have a variety of shapes. Most are round with blunt serration or indentations ④. Unlike the Silver Poplar (p180), the underside of the leaves, especially the younger leaves, has noticeable grey hairs.

BLOOMS: Male and female catkins are found on different plants. Both hang down limply and have a reddish colour.

TYPICAL FEATURES
The buds of the Grey Poplar ③ and the underside of the young leaves have grey, felt-like hairs.

FRUITS: The two sides of the tiny capsules burst open and release tiny seeds with white flight hairs.

DISTRIBUTION: In lowland forests.

OTHER: The Grey Poplar is the result of a natural cross-breeding of the Silver Poplar and the Aspen. It is a very undemanding plant and is normally planted in different forms as avenue trees.

London Plane

Platanus x hispanica

DESCRIPTION: The London Plane is a deciduous tree, which can reach a height of 35m and which has a broad, spreading crown and sturdy main branches ①. Its bark is smooth and flakes in large pieces ②.

LEAVES: The leaves have lobes much like the Maple ③. Each of the three to five lobes has blunt serration and ends in a point.

BLOOMS: Male and female flowers form separately in oval heads about 1cm long, which hang on stems beneath the branches.

FRUITS: The flower heads develop into spherical fruits ④.

> **TYPICAL FEATURES**
> The easiest way to identify the London Plane is by its flaking bark which gives the trunk a blotchy appearance ②.

DISTRIBUTION: The London Plane is a hybrid between the Oriental Plane Tree *(Platanus orientalis)* and the American Sycamore *(Platanus occidentalis),* but it is not known how this cross occurred. It is very common as an avenue tree and in parks.

Black Mulberry

Morus nigra

DESCRIPTION: The Black Mulberry is a 15m-high tree with a round crown. Its gnarled trunk branches at a low height into sturdy branches ①.

LEAVES: The leaves are either a broad oval with a point ② or have well-defined lobes ③. The leaf edges have rough serration.

BLOOMS: Male flowers form hanging catkins; female flowers can form on the same tree or on different trees in short-stemmed heads.

FRUITS: The individual round nuts form a fleshy, blackberry-like fruit. Its colour changes from white to red to black when ripening ④.

> **TYPICAL FEATURES**
> The leaves of the Black Mulberry take a variety of shapes and feel rough on the upper surface. The underside of the leaf has soft hairs.

DISTRIBUTION: Native to the Near East; cultivated in Central Europe and has become wild in regions with a mild climate.

OTHER: The fruits taste pleasant but sour and can be eaten raw or made into a jam or syrup.

173

European White Elm

Fluttering Elm

Ulmus laevis

DESCRIPTION: A deciduous tree reaching a height of 30m with a broad, cloud-shaped crown ①. Established trees often have vertical, plank-like extensions at the trunk base, which join the roots and provide additional support.

LEAVES: Particularly noticeable is the very asymmetric leaf base ②. The edge of the leaf is rough, with fine serration, and ends in a point.

BLOOMS: The unremarkable, stemmed flowers appear before the leaves in loose clusters, which hang from the branches ③.

TYPICAL FEATURES

European White Elm can be mistaken for the Small-leaved Elm, due to its crooked leaf-stalk. One difference is the long-stemmed flowers and fruits.

FRUITS: Nuts with broad wings ④ hang in loose fruit clusters.

DISTRIBUTION: Meadows, riverbanks, on partially flooded soil.

OTHER: The European White Elm is susceptible to a fungus, Dutch Elm Disease, which penetrates the wood. The branches of stricken trees then wither, and the tree usually dies very quickly.

Small-leaved Elm

Smooth-leaved Elm

Ulmus minor

DESCRIPTION: The Small-leaved Elm is a deciduous tree, which can reach a height of 30m, with a narrow, cloud-shaped crown ①. Young branches have hairs and a red bark; the trunk is grey-brown, with vertical fissures.

LEAVES: Stemmed leaves have an asymmetric base ③, end in a point and have serrated edges.

BLOOMS: The flowers appear before the leaves. They form dense clusters, which stand on the branches on short stems.

TYPICAL FEATURES

The young branches of the Small-leaved Elm grow on characteristic short protrusions ②.

FRUITS: The small nuts have short stems and a wing that extends around the whole circumference ④, slightly curved down at the tip.

DISTRIBUTION: In deciduous and mixed woodland and lowland forests; also on riverbanks.

OTHER: Like the European White Elm, the Small-leaved Elm is susceptible to Dutch Elm disease, which is caused by a fungus. The very useful hard wood is often used to make furniture, often as a veneer.

Sweet Chestnut
Spanish Chestnut | Edible Chestnut
Castanea sativa

DESCRIPTION: The Sweet Chestnut is a 35m-tall tree with a broad crown ①. Older trees have substantial branches near to the ground.

LEAVES: Short-stemmed, long leaves end in a point ②. Edges have rough serration, and each serrated tooth ends in a thin, thorn-like point.

BLOOMS: Male flowers form in yellow, spherical heads, arranged in rows to form a catkin up to 25cm long ③. The unremarkable female flowers form at the base of these catkins.

> **TYPICAL FEATURES**
> The long catkins and the pointed, serrrated leaves are characteristic of the Sweet Chestnut, as are the spiny fruits.

FRUITS: The fruits can be almost the size of a fist ④ and are covered in dense spines. They contain brown, leathery nuts called sweet chestnuts.

DISTRIBUTION: Native to southern Europe, Asia Minor and North Africa; cultivated in sheltered, mild regions of the United Kingdom.

OTHER: The fruits are edible when roasted or steamed.

Silver Lime | Silver Linden
Tilia tomentosa

DESCRIPTION: A deciduous tree, which can reach a height of 30m ①. Young plants have an almost spherical crown; older trees have a broad crown with vertical branches. Smaller branches have grey, felt-like hairs.

LEAVES: The round leaves have a heart-shaped indentation where the leaf joins the stem, and end in a short point. The edges are serrated and the underside of the leaf has dense white hairs ④.

> **TYPICAL FEATURES**
> The Silver Lime does not bloom until midsummer, and the flowers release an intense, sweet aroma.

BLOOMS: The yellow flowers hang in umbellate clusters from the younger branches ②. A narrow leaf grows at the base of each flower cluster.

FRUITS: The small, spherical nuts are hard and have felt-like hairs ③. The fruit clusters have a similar form to the flower clusters.

DISTRIBUTION: Native to south-east Europe and Asia Minor; planted to line streets and in gardens in the United Kingdom.

OTHER: The flowers of the Silver Lime produce large amounts of nectar, which is indigestible for European insects.

Small-leaved Lime
Common Linden
Tilia cordata

DESCRIPTION: A deciduous tree, which can reach a height of 30m. It has a short trunk and a wide crown ①. In woodland, the trunk is longer and the crown narrower. Black-grey bark ② has long, vertical furrows. Young branches usually have no hairs.

LEAVES: The stemmed, round leaves end in a short point and have a heart-shaped indentation at the stalk ③. The edge of the leaf has fine serration, and the leaf stalk has no hairs.

TYPICAL FEATURES
The Small-leaved Lime, unlike the Large-leaved Lime, has leaves which are only 3–10cm long, and the tufts of hairs on the leaf veins are a brown colour ③.

BLOOMS: Yellow flowers hang in umbellate clusters from branches. A narrow leaf forms at the base of the cluster stalk.

FRUITS: The small, spherical nuts ④ are brittle and can be easily crushed between the fingers.

DISTRIBUTION: In lowland forests and deciduous and mixed woodland, on sunny slopes.

Large-leaved Lime
Tilia platyphyllos

DESCRIPTION: The Large-leaved Lime is a deciduous tree, which can grow to a height of up to 40m. In woodland the crown remains narrow, but individual trees ① develop a broad crown. Young branches always have velvety hairs.

LEAVES: Stemmed, almost heart-shaped leaves ② have a short point and edges with pointed serration. Asymmetric at the stalk, which, unlike on the Small-leaved Lime, has hairs.

TYPICAL FEATURES
The leaves of the Large-leaved Lime can grow to 17cm. The leaf veins on the underside of the leaf have white tufts of hair ②.

BLOOMS: Greenish-yellow flowers have an intense aroma and are arranged in groups of two to five on hanging panicles ④. Narrow leaves grow where the panicle joins the branch.

FRUITS: The spherical nut fruits are light brown when ripe and have five prominent ridges running from base to tip ③. They are so hard that they cannot be compressed between two fingers.

DISTRIBUTION: In semi-shady locations in mild, humid regions and up to an altitude of 1,000m.

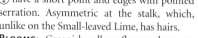

179

Black Poplar

Populus nigra

DESCRIPTION: The Black Poplar is a deciduous tree, which can grow to a height of 30m, with a broad, loose crown ①.

LEAVES: The long-stemmed leaves have an almost triangular contour and end in a long point ②. The edges have a regular, fine serration.

BLOOMS: The flowers emerge in spring before the leaves ④. The light green female catkins and the red male catkins ③ form on different plants. They are finger-length and hang loosely from the branch.

FRUITS: The round capsules form in rows on the long stalks of the female catkins. When fully developed they release numerous seeds with white flight hairs.

DISTRIBUTION: In damp woodlands; Black Poplars found in other habitats are mostly cultivated or hybrids.

TYPICAL FEATURES
The trunk of the Black Poplar has a dark grey, almost black bark, with deep, vertical fissures.

Silver Poplar

Populus alba

DESCRIPTION: The Silver Poplar is a deciduous tree, which can reach a height of 35m, with a broad, irregular crown ①. Young shoots have white, felt-like hairs, but later become bald.

LEAVES: The stemmed leaves can have a variety of forms. Some are almost oval, while others have well-defined lobes. There are also many intermediate forms. The underside of the leaf always has dense, felt-like hairs ④.

BLOOMS: Flowers appear before the leaves, male and female flowers forming on different plants. Male catkins are roughly finger-length and red; female flowers are slightly shorter and a yellow-green colour ③.

FRUITS: The tiny capsules form in hanging clusters. When ripe they release small, hairy seeds.

DISTRIBUTION: In lowland forests near large rivers; on nutrient-rich, loose soil; quite frequently planted as a park tree.

OTHER: The Silver Poplar can live for 400 years.

TYPICAL FEATURES
The smooth, light grey bark of the Silver Poplar flakes off in diamond-shaped pieces ②. The white, felt-like underside of the leaves is also characteristic.

Nettle Tree
European Hackberry | *Celtis australis*

DESCRIPTION: The Nettle Tree is deciduous and can reach a height of 25m. It forms a regular, round crown ①. The smooth, grey bark ② is slightly reminiscent of the bark of the Common Beech (p166).

LEAVES: The short-stemmed leaves are arranged in two rows on the branches. They are long and oval and have long tips ④.

BLOOMS: Unremarkable, long-stemmed flowers grow where the leaf stalk joins the branch. Flowers are single blooms, with both male and female parts, or clusters of just male flowers.

TYPICAL FEATURES

The leaves of the Nettle Tree have a long, slightly bent tip. The upper surface of the leaf feels rough, and the underside has soft hairs.

FRUITS: The stone fruits have a diameter of about 1cm and hang on long stems ③. When ripe they are red-brown to almost black.

DISTRIBUTION: Southern Europe, North Africa, Near Asia; rare in the United Kingdom. In South Tyrol, the tree is cultivated for its edible fruits (hackberries).

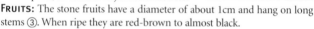

Wych Elm
Ulmus glabra

DESCRIPTION: The Wych Elm is a deciduous tree, which can reach a height of 40m ①. It forms a broad, overhanging crown. The grey-brown bark has vertical fissures.

LEAVES: The oval leaves are asymmetric at the stalk. The edges are indented and finely serrated. Two of the serrated teeth near the tip of the leaf and one at the tip are normally larger than the rest and point forward ④.

TYPICAL FEATURES

The Wych Elm is the only Elm with three-pointed leaves, which are rough and hairy on both sides.

BLOOMS: The tiny flowers emerge before the leaves. They form in large numbers in reddish clusters ② on the branches.

FRUITS: The nut fruits ripen by late spring. The long seeds are located in the centre of a green, oval wing ③.

DISTRIBUTION: In deciduous and mixed woodland in gorges and on slopes; at mid-altitude in low mountain ranges, and up to an altitude of about 1,400m.

OTHER: Wych Elms can live for 400 years. They are also susceptible to Dutch Elm Disease.

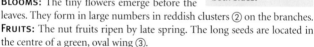

183

Sessile Oak
Quercus petraea

DESCRIPTION: The Sessile Oak is a deciduous tree, which can reach a height of 40m ①. The trunk runs straight up through the tree, almost to the tip of the regular, fanning crown. The bark of older trees is very thick, grey-brown and has long, deep fissures.

TYPICAL FEATURES

The Sessile Oak has a long, straight trunk, and leaves with relatively long stalks.

LEAVES: Stemmed, oval leaves become narrower near the stalk. Edges have rounded indentations ②. Corners of leaf veins on the underside of the leaf have small tufts of hairs.

BLOOMS: The male flowers form in large numbers in hanging catkins ③; female flowers form in unremarkable clusters.

FRUITS: The acorns are 2–3cm long, with almost no stalk, and sit on the branches ④. The acorn cups only cover the bottom third of the fruit.

DISTRIBUTION: Deciduous woods, from sea-level to low mountain ranges.

OTHER: The nutritious fruits used to be used as fodder for pigs, which were taken to woodlands in herds.

Common Oak
Quercus robur

DESCRIPTION: The Common Oak can grow to a height of 40m, with an overhanging, irregular crown ①. The trunk divides into several main branches at a low level, and does not run through the tree like that of the Sessile Oak.

TYPICAL FEATURES

The trunk of the Common Oak branches at a low level. The bark has deep furrows ②.

LEAVES: The short-stemmed leaves have deep indentations, but they are not symmetrical ③. Where the leaf joins the stalk, there are often small, ear-like protrusions.

BLOOMS: The male flowers hang limply from the branches in yellow-green catkins; the female flowers are brown and spherical and form in groups of between two and five on long stalks at the ends of the branches.

FRUITS: The 2–3cm-long acorns hang on long stems from the branches ④. The acorn cups are very flat.

DISTRIBUTION: Deciduous and mixed woodland, from sea-level to low mountain ranges.

185

Index

190

Acknowledgements

Cover: Oak; small pictures from left to right: Birch, White Oak, Yew
Page 6/7: Large-leaved Lime   **Page 24/25:** Wild Cherry

blickwinkel/Stenner: Page U2 r. mi., 14 top, 67 top r., 157 top l.;
blickwinkel/Tomm: Page 145 top r.;
blickwinkel/Westerwinter: Page 53 top r.;
Getty Images: Page U 1 top l.;
Himmelhuber: Page 67 bot. r., 91 bot., 105 bot. l., 111 bot. l., 113 bot. r., 169 top r.;
Janke: Page 111 bot. r.;
Kremer: Page 181 top l.;
Laux: Page U 1 top mi., 9 bot., 12 bot., 17 mi. bot., bot., 21 bot. mi. l., 27 bot., 29 top, 35 bot. l., 41 bot. r., 43 bot. l., 53 top l., bot. l., 55 top l., bot. l., 57 top l., top r., bot. l., 67 bot. l., 71 top l., 83 top l., 87 top r., 91 top l., 93 top l., top r., 95 top r., bot. l., bot. r., 99 top l., top r., 101 top l., 107 top l., bot. r., 109, 113 top l., top r., 115 bot. r., 117 bot. l., 119 bot. l., bot. r., 121 top l., bot. l., 123 top l., 125 top, 127 top l., 129 top l., 131 top r., 133 top l., 135 top l., bot. l., bot. r., 141 top l., bot. r., 143 top r., 145 top l., 147 top r., 149 top l., 151 top l., top r., bot. l., 155 top r., bot. r., 173 bot. l., 175 bot. r., 177 bot. r., U 4 r.;
Marktanner: Page 13 l. mi., 15 bot., 35 top l., 63 bot. r., 87 bot. l., bot. r., 89 bot. r., 99 bot. l., 117 bot. r., 135 top r.;
Pforr, E.: Page 22 bot., 83 o., 85 bot. l., bot. r., 93 bot. r.;
Pforr, M.: Page U 1 top r., U 2 l. mi., l. bot., r. top, r. bot., 3, 10, 12 top, mi., 13 l. bot., r. top, r. bot., 14 bot. l., bot. mi., 15 top, 16 bot. l., bot. mi., bot. r., 17 top, mi. top, 19 l. top, 21 l., bot. mi. r., 22 top, 23, 27 top l., 27 bot., 29 top l., bot., bot. r., 31 bot. r., 35 top l., 37 top r., 39 bot. r., 47 top l., 51 top r., 55 top, bot. r., 57 bot. r., 59 top r., 65 top r., 69 top r., bot., 71 top r., bot. l., bot. r., 73 top r., 75 top r., 77 top l., top r., bot. r., 79 top r., 81 top r., 83 bot. r., 85 top l., 87 top l., 89 bot. l., 91 bot. r., 97 top l., top r., 101 bot. l., bot. r., 103 top l., 107 top, 115 top r., bot. l., 119 top l., 121 top r., bot. r., 123 top r., bot. r., 125 top l., 125 bot. r., 127 bot. r., 129 bot., bot. r., 131 bot. l., 137 top, bot. l., bot. r., 139 top r., bot. r., 143 bot. l., bot. r., 145 bot. l., bot. r., 147 bot. l., bot. r., 149 top r., bot. r., 151 bot. r., 153 top l., 157 top r., 159 top l., bot. l., bot. l., 161 bot. l., bot. r., 163 bot. r., 165 bot. l., 167 top l., 169 bot. r., 175 top l., 177 top l., bot. l., 179 bot. r., 181 top r., 185 top l., top r., bot. l.;
Reinhard, H.: Page 49 top l., 59 bot. l., bot. r., 61 bot. r., 63 top l., top r., 79 bot. r., 89 top l., top r., 111 top l., 113 bot. l., 117 top l., top r., 123 bot. l., 131 top l., bot. l., 133 bot. l., bot. r., 157 bot. l., bot. r., 175 bot. l.;
Reinhard, N.: Page 61 bot., 111 top r.;
Riedmiller: Page U 2 l. top, 8, 9 top, mi., 13 l. top, r. mi., 14 bot. r., 18, 19 r. top, 21 top, bot. l., bot. r., 27 top, 31 top l., 33, 35 bot. r., 37 top l., bot. l., 39 top l., top r., bot. l., 41 top, top l., bot., 43 top r., top r., bot. r., 45, 47 top r., bot. l., bot. r., 49 bot. l., bot. r., 51 top l., bot. l., bot. r., 59 top l., bot. r., 65 top l., bot. r., 69 top l., bot. l., bot. r., 73 top l., bot. l., bot. r., 75 top l., bot. r., 77 bot. l., 79 bot. l., 81 bot. r., 83 bot., 85 top, 97 bot. l., 103 top r., bot. l., bot. r., 105 top r., bot. r., 125 bot. l., 127 top r., 129 top, 133 top r., 137 top l., 139 top l., 141 top r., bot. l., 147 top l., 149 bot. r., 153 bot. r., 155 bot. l., 159 top l., top r., bot. r., 165 top r., bot. r., 167 bot., bot. r., 169 bot. l., 171, 173 top l., top r., 179 top r., top l., 181 bot. r., bot. r., 183, 185 bot. r.;
Seidl: Page 49 o., 53 bot. l., 95 top l., 115 top l., 169 top l.;
Willner, O.: Page 61 top l., 75 bot. l., 105 top l., 139 bot. l.;
Willner, W.: Page 2, 6/7, 15 mi., 16 o., 19 l. bot., r. bot., 20 mi. l., mi. r., 24/25, 31 bot. l., bot. r., 61 o., 63 bot. l., 65 top l., 67 top l., 69 top r., 79 top l., 81 top l., bot. l., 91 o., 93 bot., 99 bot. r., 101 top r., 119 top r., 127 bot., 143 top l., 153 top r., bot. r., 155 top l., 161 top l., top r., 165 top l., 167 top r., 173 bot. r., 175 top r., 177 top r., U 4 m.;
ZEFA/Kalt: Page U1 (large picture).

Acknowledgements

The dates and facts in this nature guide have been researched and checked with great care. No guarantee can, however, be given, and the publisher accepts no liability for damage to people, property or assets.

This edition first published in 2006 by New Holland Publishers (UK) Ltd
London • Cape Town • Sydney • Auckland
10 9 8 7 6 5 4 3 2 1
www.newhollandpublishers.com
Garfield House, 86–88 Edgware Road, London, W2 2EA, UK

ISBN 1 84537 475 4

Publishing Manager: Jo Hemmings
Senior Editor: Kate Michell
Assistant Editor: Kate Parker
Translator: American Pie, London and California

Series Editor: Steffen Haselbach
Editor-in-chief: Anita Zellner
Desk Editors: Dr. Michael Eppinger, Dr. Helga Hofmann
Cover design: independent Medien-Design
Layout: H. Bornemann Design
Illustrations: Peter Braun, atelier amAldi
Film: Filmsatz Schröter, Munich
Production: Petra Roth
Repro: Penta, München
Printing: Appl, Wemding
Binding: Auer, Donauwörth
Printed in Germany